HOW TO LIVE LIKE A MONK

Danièle Cybulskie

Illustrations by Anna Lobanova

HOW TO LIVE
LIKE A
MONK

Medieval Wisdom
for
Modern Life

Abbeville Press Publishers
New York   London

*This book is dedicated to the memory of
my great-grandmother, Freda Horton, a
woman who was equal parts pithy wisdom,
fashion savvy, courage, and love.*

—Danièle Cybulskie

Project Editor: Lauren Bucca
Copy Editor: Amy K. Hughes
Design: Misha Beletsky
Production Manager: Louise Kurtz

Copyright © 2021 Abbeville Press. All rights reserved under
international copyright conventions. No part of this book may
be reproduced or utilized in any form or by any means, electronic
or mechanical, including photocopying, recording, or by any
information retrieval system, without permission in writing from
the publisher. Inquiries should be addressed to Abbeville Press,
655 Third Avenue, New York, NY 10017. The text of this book was set
in Study. Printed in China.

First edition
10 9 8 7 6 5 4 3 2 1

Library of Congress Cataloging-in-Publication Data
Names: Cybulskie, Danièle, author. Title: How to live like a monk :
medieval wisdom for modern life / Danièle Cybulskie. Description:
First edition. | New York : Abbeville Press Publishers, [2021] |
Includes bibliographical references and index. | Summary:
"A book on how medieval monastic practices can inspire us
to live fuller lives"—Provided by publisher.
Identifiers: LCCN 2021023864 | ISBN 9780789214133
Subjects: LCSH: Monastic and religious life.
Classification: LCC BX2435 .C93 2021 | DDC 248.8/9432—dc23
LC record available at https://lccn.loc.gov/2021023864

For bulk and premium sales and for text adoption procedures,
write to Customer Service Manager, Abbeville Press,
655 Third Avenue, New York, NY 10017, or call 1-800-ARTBOOK.

Visit Abbeville Press online at www.abbeville.com.

The Five-Minute Medievalist logo by Eric Overton

Contents

AD REGULAM

Carry out this little Rule sketched as a beginning, and then at last you will reach ... greater heights of learning and virtues.

—Benedict of Nursia, *The Rule of Saint Benedict*

his book was dreamed up well before COVID-19 became a global pandemic, forcing so many of us to temporarily retreat into living cloistered lives like monks, as it were. However, the social isolation that came with this most recent pandemic served to make clearer, perhaps, both the reasons monastic living has appealed to so many over the last two millennia and why—and how—it worked in the Middle Ages, the thousand-year period between roughly 500 CE and 1500 CE.

The earliest people who practiced what would evolve into Christian monastic living were the desert hermits

Although some hermits, like Saint Anthony (left, pictured with Saint Jerome), were able to lead spiritual lives on their own, monastic communities were developed to make it easier to avoid temptation.

The Almugavar Hours, fol. 276v, c. 1510–20 (detail)

Walters Art Museum, Baltimore; W.420

of late antiquity, who left society as completely as possible in order to spend all their time in religious contemplation. Those hermits, as their biographies tell us, fought hard against the forces of the devil to keep themselves living what they saw as pure and virtuous lives. They were upheld by many as the pinnacle of piety, and several of them, like Saint Anthony, attaining sainthood.

As the isolation that came with 2020 taught so many of us, however, it can be hard to resist temptation when you're all alone. From the sourdough bread experiments that tempted us to delicious gluttony to the Netflix binges that tempted us to sloth, we rediscovered that being alone sometimes makes it extremely difficult to keep to our resolutions, no matter how firmly we wish to and no matter how deep our desire to do well.

Early Christians (like those of other faiths both before and since) recognized that sometimes there is strength in numbers when it comes to individual temptation, and so they began to create communities of people who wanted to follow the path of righteousness but needed the help and the support of other people to do it to the best of their ability. Basically, they decided to be hermits together. With this, the first Christian monasteries were born.

Monastic life has changed shape over the course of nearly two millennia, as individual monks, communities, and popes wrestled with the challenges that come with dozens—or even hundreds—of people attempting to be hermits together and to live without sin. European monastic life was at its most iconic during the medieval period, so it is to those brothers and sisters we'll turn for our inspiration on how to live like a monk.

If you're interested in committing yourself to a monastic community to serve the will of God with your whole heart and soul, this is probably not the book for you. It seems safe to say, though, that many yearn for peace, simplicity, and purpose in our lives, and these are some of the principles around which the monastic path was created. So, for those of us who wish to live *like* monks, not *as* monks, read on for some ways in which the monastic life of the European Middle Ages can help us to live *ad regulam*—toward a rule that's of our own making, in tune with our own goals and values.

To take the solitary path of the hermitage or anchor-hold was to face a great deal of demonic temptation without the spiritual aid of a community.
The Smithfield Decretals, fol. 113v, late 13th–early 14th century (detail)
British Library, London; Royal 10 E IV

What Is a Monk?

> *When a man goeth alone in a slippery path, he soon*
> *slides and falls; and when many go together and every*
> *one has hold of another's hand, if any of them begin to*
> *slide, the next one pulls him up before he quite fall; and if*
> *they grow weary, every one is supported by another.*
> —*The Ancren Riwle*

Before we decide if we want to live like monks, it seems wise to actually establish what one *is*.[1] There were many different types of clergy in the medieval world, but they fell into two basic categories. First were the secular clergy, who did their work in the greater community. They included priests, chaplains, and bishops, as well as the clergy who worked in secular (as in, not religious) jobs, like clerks and scribes. The second category was regular clergy; that is, those who followed a rule (from the Latin *regula*, as in "regulations"). These were normally people who lived in enclosed communities, such as monks and nuns, but also included mendicant (begging) orders, like the friars who would wander around preaching and begging for food. The mendicant orders included Franciscans, Dominicans, and Augustinians. Friar Tuck, of Robin Hood fame, had a tonsure and wore robes, but as a friar, he lived *in* the world, not apart from it. He was therefore not a monk. Although members of the military orders, such as the Templars and the Hospitallers, also took vows and obeyed rules, they were not considered monks either. These are technical terms, however, and plenty of friars spent most—if not all—of their time enclosed instead of on the road. As we'll soon see, a detailed source from an English house of Augustinians gives us a clear view into life for religious brothers who chose to stay within the monastery's walls.

The Rule of Saint Benedict
(compiled in the sixth century
by Benedict of Nursia, pictured)
was followed by the vast majority
of monastic houses in Europe, to
varying degrees of strictness.
Benedictional of Æthelwold, fol. 99v,
c. 963–84 (detail)
British Library, London; Additional 49598

Many large monasteries housed both monks and nuns,
although they were not permitted to socialize with each other.
The Queen Mary Psalter, fol. 176v, 1310–20 (detail)
British Library, London; Royal 2 B VII

Abbesses, like the famous Héloïse (left), were powerful and influential figures beyond the walls of their abbeys because of their wisdom and administrative abilities.

Art d'Amour, fol. 137r, late 15th century (detail)
British Library, London; Royal 16 F II

Within their enclosed communities, monks and nuns followed a set of rules that dictated everything from when to pray to when to eat, to how to discipline unruly brothers. Usually, they followed three basic principles: poverty, chastity, and obedience. Most medieval monks followed

The Rule of Saint Benedict, written by Benedict of Nursia, an abbot in Montecassino, Italy, in the sixth century, and widely spread as the gold standard for monastic living during the rule of Charlemagne (c. 747–814). Those houses that followed this rule closely were Benedictines, but there were other monastic orders that followed Saint Benedict with some tweaks, such as the Cistercians and Cluniacs.

These days, the word "monastery" is used almost exclusively for a male-only house of religious people, but in the Middle Ages, it was used interchangeably for houses of both monks and nuns. In fact, there were more than a few monastic houses in medieval Europe that had communities of *both* monks and nuns within the same grounds—separated by gender, of course—often under the care of an abbess, like the famous Fontevraud Abbey in France, the final resting place of Richard the Lionheart and his mother, Eleanor of Aquitaine.

Monks and nuns followed basically the same rules, with some exceptions. For example, no matter how holy a nun was, she was not permitted to be ordained as a priest. That meant that every community of nuns was still de-

Nuns also followed The Rule of Saint Benedict *and were ruled over by an abbess.*

Omne Bonum (Absolucio-Circumcisio), fol. 27r, c. 1360–75 (detail)
British Library, London; Royal 6 E VI

pendent on having regular visits by priests to perform their Masses, deliver sermons, and take their confessions.

For the purposes of this book, we'll go with "monk" and "monastery" most of the time for simplicity's sake, but it's worth remembering that communities of female religious lived very similar lives.

Why Become a Monk?

> *The occasions of conversion are many…but the greatest numbers are converted by the ministry of others, as by the word of exhortation, or the power of prayer, or the example of a Religious life.*
> —Caesarius of Heisterbach, *The Dialogue on Miracles*

Popular culture would have us believe that there were only two paths to the monastery: you were either extremely devout, or you were a younger child who was unlikely to inherit and therefore must be given to the church. In reality, there were many roads that led to the doors of the abbey.

In the Middle Ages, the church was where boys were given an education, especially if their families were not rich enough to hire them private tutors. Boys who were

A monastic education gave boys a variety of career options, both in the church and outside of it.
Scholastic miscellany, fol. 288v, 1309–16 (detail)
British Library, London; Burney 275

Boys given to the monastery to be raised there were called oblates.
Decretum, fol. 82v, late 13th century (detail)
British Library, London; Royal 10 D VIII

raised with a formal education could grow up to fill a religious post or a secular post such as doctor or lawyer, which would give them a good or steady income. Sending your child to a monastery for education wasn't quite the ritual sacrifice it may look like in media representations, through which parents were hoping for divine favor (although it certainly couldn't hurt a person's chances in the afterlife), but an opportunity for that child to go places in the world. Children who were sent to a monastery for life were called oblates.

While oblates were a part of the monastic tradition for quite a long time, not everyone approved of having children in the monastery: they're noisy and disruptive, playful when they should be serious, and require a lot of attention and care that the monks could be spending on their pious works. People were also uneasy about having children devoted to a monastic life before they were old enough to choose for themselves, so eventually it was made official that oblates could leave the monastery if they wished, instead of taking vows in their late teens. Some children ended up in monasteries (either temporarily or permanently) under different circumstances. For example, people without the resources or ability to care for children might abandon them anonymously at the monastery gates to be cared for by the community. There were also some exceptions made, such as in the case of Edward I of England's daughter Mary, who was sent to a convent at the age of six to be a companion to her grandmother, Eleanor of Provence.[2]

Monasteries' close links with literacy and education were a good reason for adults to take vows too. Many an educated lady who had been widowed, as Eleanor of Provence was, chose to retire to a monastery or convent in order to spend her days with like-minded women, reading and studying. The same went for men who wanted to spend their twilight years in a retirement that was relatively comfortable and gave them the opportunity to set themselves right with God before their deaths. Some people took vows to atone for a grievous sin they'd committed, and others were unintentionally made members of a monastic community, having fled to an abbey for sanctuary to avoid punishment for a crime. Sanctuary seekers could not set foot outside the sacred ground of the abbey without a pardon or a promise to head directly into exile, and conviction for a crime such as theft, rape, or murder could easily result in capital punishment. Members of urban monasteries such as London's Westminster Abbey, then, could often have the unexpected pleasure of

Nuns also received educations in the abbey, and many widowed noblewomen retired there, in part to continue to read and learn.

Prayer book, fol. 26v, early 16th century (detail)
Walters Art Museum, Baltimore; W.432

the company of criminals, who had no choice but to become members (either lay or full) of the community, or face death or exile.[3]

There were, of course, those who took monastic vows out of sincere devotion, too, and this accounts for the majority of people within monastic communities across Europe, as Caesarius suggests, even if this makes for less salacious reading. Medieval theology dictated that becoming a monk or nun was one of the best ways to serve God: to devote your life to his service, giving up all fleshly pleasures and worldly ambitions. Living according to strict rules was definitely not easy, which is exactly what made it an extraordinary and praiseworthy act of love and devotion.

How Did a Person Become a Monk?

> If the novice be able and willing chiefly for the sake
> of God, to endure with a good heart nocturnal vig-
> ils, a dull life in the Cloister, continual services in the
> Quire [choir], prolonged silence, the strictness of the
> Order and of the particular house, and the different
> characters of the brethren…leave should be given
> him to profess at the end of the year.
> —*Observances* of Barnwell Priory

Because monastic living required a lot from a person—
humility, patience, and hard work, among other
things—people had to go through a trial period (novitiate)
before they could take their vows. This trial run usually
lasted a year, during which the person had to live as the
other brothers lived but was still free to leave if he chose.

*A monk's novitiate was generally one year long, in order to
give him time to decide whether monastic life really was
for him. Only one of these novices has decided to take his
monastic vows, while the other has had second thoughts.*
Decretum, fol. 201r, late 13th century (detail)
British Library, London; Royal 10 D VIII

Monks held onto novices' street clothes until they took their vows, in case they decided not to stay. After a novice had professed, his clothes were donated to charity.
Decretum, fol. 213v, late 13th–early 14th century (detail)
British Library, London; Royal 11 D IX

When a person entered the monastery, he gave up his street clothes and shoes (put aside in case he changed his mind later) and took on the robes of a monk. His duties were not as arduous as a fully avowed monk's were, and his clothing was slightly more comfortable. Novices were separated from the monks as much as possible, in order to keep distractions to the brothers to a minimum, and they were not permitted to be part of the discussion of monastic business that occurred every day in the chapter house.

Each novice was assigned a master who would teach him his prayers (in Latin), the psalms, and the rules of the monastery. Fortunately for us, the brothers of Barnwell Priory, an Augustinian house in England, left a detailed record of daily life there, and their description of the training required for a novice gives us an unexpected window into what was important for him to know.[4] At Barnwell, this started with the basics:

> At first then the master will teach the novice how he is to arrange his habit about him when he stands, and when he sits; secondly, how he ought to bow low in such a way that his hands when crossed may reach to his knees, and how at every bow he may, by means of

> both hands, make the sign of the cross in front of him
> with his habit. Thirdly, let the master teach him how
> to keep guard over his eyes.[5]

As this excerpt illustrates, there was more to monastic life than just memorizing prayers: it was an entire world of rituals and rules for a new brother to immerse himself in. To commit his life to the cloister was to agree to perform these motions all day, every day, for the rest of his life.

Before he took his vows, the novice might spend the night, or even several nights, in relative solitude and prayer, reflecting on his decision, as it was extremely rare for anyone to be released from his monastic vows once he took them. During this time, he was often hooded and relegated to the back of the choir during services.

When the novice took his vows, he dedicated himself to obedience to his abbot in all things—even if he disagreed—and promised to be true to his vows of poverty and chastity for the rest of his life. He was to put this in writing, using only his name, or a mark if he was illiterate. He was then unhooded, given his tonsure (the shaved

Clergymen of all types were identifiable by their tonsures, circular shaved patches at the crowns of their heads.

Life of Guthlac, roundel 3, late 12th–early 13th century (detail)
British Library, London; Harley Y 6

patch at the top of a monk's head), and welcomed as a full brother with the kiss of peace and Communion. From then on, the new monk was to devote his heart and soul to God, through all difficulty and all doubt. His world had shrunk down to a space of a few buildings enclosed by a stone wall.

What Did a Monastery Look Like?

If possible, the monastery should be set up so that all necessities—that is, water, a mill, a garden, are inside the monastic compound and various crafts can be practiced there, so there is no need for monks to roam outside, which is not at all beneficial for their souls.
—Benedict of Nursia, *The Rule of Saint Benedict*

Because we think of a monk's life as being devoted to prayer, it can be hard to imagine his orbit as being bigger than the four walls of the church itself. When we start to think about the ways in which a monastery had to support itself, however, the list of necessary buildings becomes very long indeed.

Monasteries took up huge swaths of land in many cases, so that the monks would have enough space to live, work, worship, and produce the food they needed to sustain themselves. Some monasteries relied on trade with the community or tenant farms for food, but other monasteries (such as Cistercian houses) believed they should be as self-sufficient as possible, which meant a lot of space devoted to food and workshops.

The basic buildings common to all monasteries were a church, a dormitory, and a refectory (dining hall). Sometimes dormitories and refectories could share the same architectural footprint, as a dormitory could be built on top of a refectory in a neat, two-story building. Saint Benedict

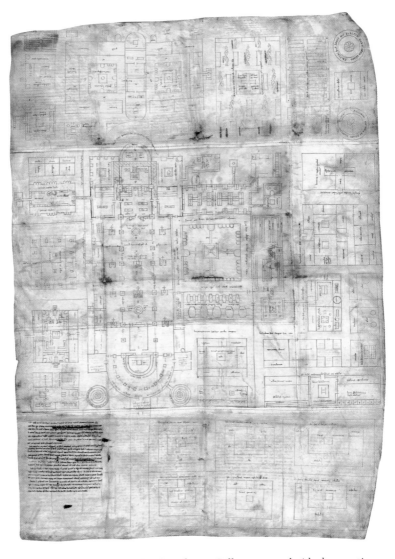

Although never built, the Plan of Saint Gall represents the ideal monastic layout, with the church and cloister in the center and buildings for guests, schooling, and storage surrounding them. The plan also includes a cemetery, a mill, and several brewhouses and bakehouses to support the community.

Codex Sangallensis, 1092r, c. 9th century
Abbey Library of Saint Gall, Saint Gallen, Switzerland

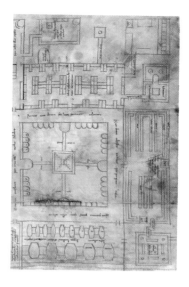

The cloister of Saint Gall was meant to contain a two-story building featuring a warming room below and dormitory above (the long rectangle at the top, which has beds drawn in). A communal privy (top right) and bathroom are attached. The refectory (right) is attached to the monks' kitchen (bottom right) and cellar (bottom left). These buildings enclose a central garth with walking paths for the brothers laid out in the shape of a cross.

Codex Sangallensis, 1092r,
c. 9th century (detail)
Abbey Library of Saint Gall, Saint Gallen, Switzerland

envisioned that all the brothers would sleep in the same long room; however, as the Middle Ages went on, monks increasingly had their own cells. Brothers were instructed to keep their doors unlocked, though, to prevent any hidden sinning.[6]

Many modern people imagine that medieval hygiene habits left a lot to be desired, but this is definitely not true, and in any case, even holy people need to relieve themselves. For this reason, monasteries frequently had privies attached to the dormitory, and some of them had running water to flush waste. Like pretty much everything else in monastic life, using the privy was anything but private; rather than individual stalls, the brothers employed rows of holes to perform their bodily functions. Because the body was considered sinful and tempting, however, monks were meant to keep their bodies as concealed as possible, to the point of covering their heads with their hoods while using the facilities.

Beyond those particular basics of hygiene, monasteries also had bathhouses. *The Rule of Saint Benedict* begrudges baths as a necessity, Saint Benedict believing they would make a man soft. Only the sick were to have frequent baths to help them recover; everyone else was to have regularly scheduled baths. Saint Benedict also stipulates that young men and older men were not to bathe together, presumably because the young men might prove too much temptation. Washing wasn't exclusive to baths, either: monks were required to wash their hands and faces when they woke up, before meals, and before they entered the church. This made for a lot of handwashing throughout the day.

Added to privies and bathhouses was a chapter house, which was the meeting place for the community to get together and discuss the day's business every morning. This was the place where the abbot would hand out work assignments, tools, or library books, where brothers could air their grievances and the misdeeds of others, and where they'd gather for emergency meetings or elections or to be addressed by a visitor.

As time went on, most monasteries included a separate suite of rooms for the abbot, including a bedroom and a parlor in which he could entertain visitors or have private chats with members of his flock. Sometimes the abbot would have his own kitchen as well. This was not only to separate the abbot because of his status as the head of the monastery but also to allow him to conduct his secular business, such as running the monastery's estates or building relationships with other landowners, without disrupting or distracting the other monks.

Monasteries also included infirmaries, where the sick and elderly would be cared for and kept warm, as there were few fires elsewhere on the grounds, in order to discourage comfort and sloth. There was sometimes a separate "warming room" with a fireplace, where everyone else could spend a few minutes in between prayers or chores. There was also often a scriptorium (the place where monks would copy books), a library, and a mill, as well as kitchens, bakehouses, breweries, laundry facilities, and storehouses.

Monasteries weren't just concerned with the monks themselves, however. One of their most important mandates was to host guests: travelers, pilgrims, family, and members of the wider religious community who might be visiting on business. This meant that there was a need for additional housing apart from where the monks lived,

Monks often had lay brothers or servants, like this unusual fellow, to help them with their tasks.

Pèlerinage de vie humaine, fol. 32r, late 14th–early 15th century (detail)
British Library, London; Harley 4399

including bedrooms, dining halls, kitchens, and privies, as well as those things that might not be needed for normal life in the monastery but were definitely necessary for guests: stables, coach houses, and sometimes even kennels.

Some of the most self-sustaining monasteries had places for lay brothers and sisters (basically support staff who lived and worked in the monastery but did not take the same vows) to sleep and eat, as well as workshops to accommodate their individual skills, from shoemaking to smithing.

When we throw in the land required to feed so many people—including kitchen gardens, medicinal gardens, crops, orchards, apiaries, pastures, fishponds, and sometimes deer parks and rabbit warrens—we get a better picture of how sprawling monastic grounds could be.

A Day in the Life of a Monk

> The Lord expects that we should daily answer these
> his sacred admonitions with deeds.
> —Benedict of Nursia, The Rule of Saint Benedict

Monastic days were divided up, as we might imagine, by set times for prayer. These set times and prayers were called the canonical hours, and they began shortly after midnight, with services every few hours until after dark. The canonical hours are probably best known today by their individual names: matins, lauds, prime, terce, sext, none, vespers, and compline. Because monks were expected to get up in the night to pray, many monasteries, like Kirkstall Abbey, a Cistercian house near Leeds, England, had "night stairs" that went directly from the monks' dormitory into the church. This opportunity to roll out of bed and down into the sanctuary seems like a rare kindness for the Cistercian brothers, who purpose-fully built their lives around austere conditions in order to better serve God.

Monks' days were devoted to prayer—both spoken and sung—manual labor, and (as we'll see later) reading. Al-though most monastic houses followed *The Rule of Saint Benedict*, there was wide variety in the way each monastic group actually practiced the rule. In accordance with their commitment to simplicity, Cistercians kept their liturgy scaled back, while Cluniacs extended their divine offices by so much that most of their day was taken up just sing-ing and chanting, leaving the lion's share of their day-to-day work to their lay brothers. Most monastic houses, of course, fell somewhere in the middle.

In the monastery, everyone had a job to do and was ex-pected to do it well, quietly, and without complaint. Of course, human nature being what it is, there was defi-nitely grumbling. Hand-copied manuscripts from the

A large part of the monastic day was spent chanting and singing.
The Huth Psalter, fol. 103v,
late 13th century (detail)
British Library, London; Additional 38116

Monks were not required to have the entire year's worth of services memorized but could read the less familiar songs and passages. Musical notation in the form we know it today was first established in the Middle Ages.
The Stowe Breviary, fol. 195v, c. 1322–25 (detail)
British Library, London; Stowe 12

Middle Ages, for example, sometimes contain scribbled complaints about abbots, the cold, or cramped hands. There were some fixed positions to which members of the community were appointed or elected, such as the sacrist (who woke the monks and kept the accoutrements of the Mass in good condition) or the cellarer (in charge of food and drink), but most of the monks performed ordinary tasks, which they would rotate on a duty roster. For example, monks took turns being the servers or the readers at mealtimes.

Monks were given two meals a day in summer and one substantial meal per day in winter. Since the canonical hours weren't fixed moments in the day but were adjusted to meet the rising and the setting of the sun, the monks needed more nourishment during the longer days of the summer season. As with most monastic activities, meals were communal, taken together in the refectory. Monks were seated like most medieval diners: they sat next to each other on benches, facing inward, with placements arranged according to seniority. This didn't necessarily mean that the oldest monks were seated together and the youngest seated with those their own age: for Saint Benedict, seniority was determined by the time the monk had spent in the monastery. It was possible, then, for a young man to outrank a much older man, if the former had taken vows as soon as he could have. Saint Benedict insisted that people's wisdom was not dependent on their ages and that young monks were as capable of providing good advice as their elders.

During mealtimes, monks were expected to stay silent and listen to a brother read from a spiritually educational book, whether it was scripture or the writings of the church fathers. Like other medieval diners, they shared a plate with a companion and were therefore expected to be polite in their dining habits.

Monks were required to cover their heads modestly with their hoods at specific times, including after the evening service and at funerals (pictured).

The Bedford Psalter and Hours, fol. 46r, c. 1414 and 1422 (detail)
British Library, London; Additional 42131

Although we tend to picture monks simply copying books, they had many other duties too, from related tasks, like creating the ink for the copyists to use, to maintenance duties, like repairing broken items. There was food to grow and prepare, guests and animals to tend, laundry to be done, and general upkeep to be performed. Specialized tasks like beekeeping, brewing, and carving could also be done by the brothers. If the daily tasks were beyond what the monks could cope with on their own between the critical times for prayer, abbeys could rely on lay brothers and sisters to share the load.

After singing and praying at the last service of the day (compline), a monk would retire to his bed in the chilly dormitory with his brethren, his hood pulled up to keep him warm and modest, and try to catch a few hours of sleep before matins. As the other monks began to snore around him, he'd drift off with the knowledge that he'd repeat the same tasks again tomorrow.

A Quick Word about "The Word"

In the twenty-first century, it can be easy to be cynical about religion, although we certainly don't have the monopoly on that—our medieval monastic friends had their fair share of doubts too, as we'll see. We might smile at some of the anecdotes of earnest brothers' belief in miracles that stretch credulity, like those regarding miraculous cheese, or we may scoff at the worldliness of brothers creating the medieval equivalent of souvenir shops for pilgrims. Religious belief, like human nature, is complex, changeable, and in many cases flexible, and that is not necessarily a flaw.

While we'll be exploring monastic life from a historical and secular perspective, it's essential to remember that monastic life was founded—and is still founded—on genuine faith and devotion to a higher power and a higher purpose. Whether or not we, as modern readers, believe that each Mass sung in the name of a patron actually lessened the benefactor's time in purgatory, we need to respect the fact that medieval monks and nuns, themselves, did; that their decisions and routines and rituals were not arbitrary but thoroughly considered, built on a foundation of faith that went back many generations over hundreds of years. We also need to remember that these were human beings whose faith fluctuated, who loved scandal and gossip, who found temptation hard to resist, and who agonized over their sinful natures and the state of their souls. They also dedicated their lives to service, and if it wasn't for their diligent and conscientious copying, we'd have a serious lack of sources from this time. We owe a lot to medieval monks as copyists, as chroniclers, and as inventors; as keepers of knowledge and as disseminators of that knowledge. As we learn how to live like monks on our own terms, we owe it to them to always be mindful and respectful of the beliefs and principles upon which they built their lives.

TEND YOUR PLANTS, AND YOUR SOUL

*Green, above all colours,
is most agreeable to the eyes.*
—*The Ancren Riwle*

n the beginning, there was a garden. For medieval Christians, the Garden of Eden is where human life, human goodness, and human strife all began. It was where humankind was at its most perfect and where everything was in balance and glory.

For the medieval monk, green space represented peace, serenity, and a return to humanity's origins. It also represented healing and nourishment, not only for the soul but also for the body. To live like a monk, then, is to respect and make use of those plants that monks believed were placed here for our purposes and the natural processes that make both gardens and people flourish and grow.

Find Yourself a Soul Patch

> *Nothing refreshes the sight so much as fine short grass.*
> —Albertus Magnus

Modern doctors have toyed with the idea of giving prescriptions for physical activity and time outdoors, but this is not a new idea. For medieval monks, whose prayers kept them within the church for a large part of the day, having time outside was considered essential. Although monks didn't wallow in the dark—they had windows and candles and lamps, of course—there is no replacement for the outdoors. And it couldn't be just a cobblestone courtyard either; it had to be green. According to Hugh of Fouilloy, "The green turf which is in the middle of the material cloister refreshes encloistered eyes and their desire to study returns. It is truly the nature of the colour green that it nourishes the eyes and preserves their vision." Another medieval writer, William of Auvergne, declared this was because green is "half way between black which dilates the eye and white which contracts it."[1]

Cloisters were arranged in squares around a central courtyard or garth—a place in which plants were grown and fountains were kept. Framing the garth were roofed, colonnaded-stone corridors for monks to walk along, under which they could take refuge from sun and rain. But in order to both accommodate foot traffic and provide the healing green the brothers needed, the garth itself was often a grass lawn. Albertus Magnus, a thirteenth-century Dominican bishop, provides a surprisingly detailed look at the effort required to create a green space of such serenity:

Garths provided green space in the center of the cloister to allow monks to refresh themselves in nature and to walk with other brethren.

Column base, c. 1130–40
The Met Cloisters, New York

One must clear the space destined for a pleasure garden of all roots, and this can hardly be achieved unless the roots are dug out, the surface levelled as much as possible, and boiling water is poured over the surface, so that the remaining roots and seeds which lie in the ground are destroyed and cannot germinate.... The ground must then be covered with turves cut from good [meadow] grass, and beaten down with wooden mallets, and stamped down well with the feet until they are hardly to be seen. Then little by little the grass pushes through like fine hair and covers the surface like a fine cloth.[2]

As a fitting metaphor of the kind that monks loved best, creating the lawn involved removing those obstacles that would harm it, transplanting new growth in their stead, and tending the grass with care.

The center of the garth could also hold other objects to both soothe the soul and encourage contemplation, such as a fountain, a juniper bush, or a mulberry tree. The gentle sounds of the fountain encouraged meditation on the Holy Trinity, while juniper, like so many other plants to be found within the monastery walls, was planted for both symbolic and practical purposes. Juniper is an evergreen, never sleeping, never changing, making it an ideal plant to help a brother contemplate the steadfastness of God's love. It was also useful, as its fragrant branches could be cut and dipped in holy water to sprinkle it during ceremonies. Mulberry, another practical plant as we'll soon see, symbolically represented the Crucifixion.[3]

While it's not always possible to provide ourselves with our own private lawns, fountains, or trees, it's essen-

Garths sometimes contained fountains, like this one, to encourage contemplation.

Fountain, c. 13th century
The Met Cloisters, New York

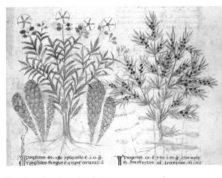

Juniper bushes (right) were a popular choice to plant in the garth, as they were both symbolic and practical.

Tractatus de herbis, fol. 49r, c. 1280–1310 (detail)
British Library, London; Egerton 747

tial for us as human beings to find ourselves with green plants before our eyes, or—even better—under our feet. Plants, besides providing us with life-giving oxygen and recycling our carbon dioxide, make us feel calm, help us fight depression, and help us recover more quickly from illness. As monks discovered, these benefits occur within minutes of us entering green space or even just looking at plants.[4] Like the monks who brought greenery into the church for something beautiful and fragrant to enhance their sacred experience (like holly or ivy for Christmas, or lilies for Easter), we can bring the outdoors into our indoor spaces to reap many of the same benefits with simple houseplants.[5] Whether we're taking a break between prayers or business meetings, it's worth giving our eyes a rest and our souls some peace by looking out a window, talking to our potted plants, or taking a short stroll across some green space.

Get Your Greens In

> *Two cooked dishes should be enough for all the brothers, and if fruit or fresh vegetables are available, they may be added as a third course. A generous pound of bread should suffice for the day, whether there is one meal or both dinner and supper.*
> —Benedict of Nursia, *The Rule of Saint Benedict*

There's a common misconception that medieval food was bland, rotten, or otherwise unappetizing, but the truth is that medieval people had access to many of the same fruits, vegetables, and herbs that we do today. Even imported spices weren't out of the reach of most monasteries, if the abbot was willing to bend Saint Benedict's rules and permit such luxuries. (The abbot himself was more likely to partake of expensive spices in his duties as host, but that privilege didn't always extend to the other brothers.)

Culinary gardens provided monks with most of the herbs we still use to make our food flavorful and fragrant today: parsley, sage, rosemary, thyme, basil, mint, and coriander (cilantro) are just a few. Some plants currently used for seasoning—like celery—were considered medicinal rather than culinary, so they didn't tend to be used in cooking. Other plants that we rarely find in modern recipes were used by medieval people to add extra flavor—herbs like lavender and flowers like roses. Saffron was frequently used in fancy dishes for both its flavor and its bright yellow color.

It was important that a monastic garden grow a variety of delicious culinary herbs, because the monastic diet was meant to be mainly vegetarian, which limited options somewhat. Monks could eat birds and fish, but according to The Rule of Saint Benedict, "they should all abstain entirely from the consumption of the meat of quadrupeds, except the gravely ill" and guests.[6] Saint Benedict wasn't sparing quadrupeds out of a sense of kindness to our animal friends exactly; meat was thought to make people lusty, as everyone in the Middle Ages had been around animals enough to have seen quadrupeds copulate at some point in their lives. Eating animals brought thoughts of animals to mind, which brought thoughts of animals mating to mind, and an entire lifetime of celibacy was difficult enough without being made to think sexy thoughts at every meal. Of course, the fact that many monasteries had extensive pastures and rabbit warrens far beyond the needs of their guests alone speaks to the fact that not every monastery kept strictly to the rules. Overweight meat-eating monks are a stereotype in stories and songs from the Middle Ages that still persists today.

Fish and other aquatic creatures were essential to the

*Monks raised many types of animals, like rabbits, to feed
their guests and sometimes themselves.*
Book of hours, fol. 96r, c. 1500 (detail)
Walters Art Museum, Baltimore; W.427

monastic diet, as fish do not mate in the same way that
humans do, and therefore looking at the fish on your
plate wasn't going to stir up any lusty images. There were
many days on which all Christians were (at least theoret-
ically) not permitted to eat meat, such as Fridays and certain holidays. In fact, many abbeys accepted eels as annual
rent payments from their tenants to get them through the
forty long fish days of Lent.[7] But monks cannot live on

The monastic diet was extremely dependent on fish and other
aquatic creatures, as Saint Benedict forbade "the meat of
quadrupeds" to all brothers, except for those who were ill.
Book of hours, fol. 2r, c. 1406–7 (detail)
British Library, London; Additional 29433

eels alone. As we all know, a balanced diet full of fruits and
vegetables is critical to good health. Fortunately, monasteries grew both.

To picture a vegetable garden in the Western world
now is to picture leafy lettuce, tomatoes, cucumbers,
and perhaps some sweet corn and even potatoes. In the
Middle Ages, however, Europe did not have sweet corn,
potatoes, or even tomatoes, as these all come from the
Americas, which—beyond a short-lived and unsuccessful
Viking settlement—hadn't yet been discovered by Europeans. Vegetable gardens in medieval Europe were full of
other things like turnips, carrots, radishes, onions, leeks,
and eggplants. Just looking at this paragraph is enough
to make the mouth water, as there is an endless variety of
ways to make tasty and filling meals out of these plants
alone.

Beyond the vegetable garden were the orchards, which
offered monks a variety of vitamin C–boosting options,
like apples, pears, and citrus, as well as other tasty offer-

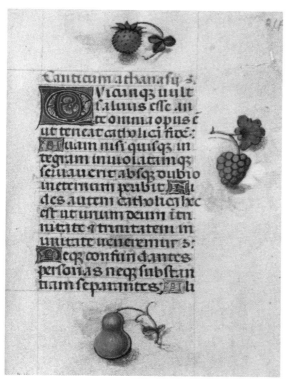

A variety of fruits, like berries, grapes, and pears, could add color and sweetness to an abbey's tables.

ings such as olives and almonds. Easier to cultivate but just as delicious were fruits such as raspberries and blackberries. Although citrus, olive, and almond trees are found mainly in southern Europe, the continent's climate during much of the Middle Ages was actually several degrees warmer than it is today, which meant that plants such as grapevines could be grown as far north as England until the fourteenth century. Monasteries cultivated vineyards too, as a way to provide their communities with both grapes and wine. Despite what you may have heard about the Middle Ages, people did drink water, but they preferred wine or ale with most meals. Wine was especially important for monasteries, given its ties to the Eucharist and association with the blood of Jesus.

The monastic diet, like pretty much all medieval diets, was heavily dependent on bread and pottage, a kind of stew or porridge made of available grains like barley and oats with any leftover tasty meat or veggies thrown in, so it contained more carbohydrates than many modern people are comfortable with. However, because medieval milling wasn't as effective as modern milling, the grains to be found within bread and pottage were coarse, full of the fiber and gut-cleaning roughage modern people get from the most expensive bakeries. Fine, white flour—the kind we now know is unhealthier—was saved for the rich.

A healthy diet for a modern person, then, isn't all that far removed from a monastic diet at the height of its late-summer plenty, with whole grains, fresh fruit and vegetables, the omega-3-boosting power of fish, and a glass of red wine. This collection of healthy foods is most commonly known as the Mediterranean diet in the modern world, and its health benefits are many, including a longer life span and a lower risk of a range of ailments like cancer, cardiovascular disease, and neuro-degenerative disease.[8] Fortunately, we now have the privilege of enjoying these options even during the coldest nights of winter, as well as to supplement our diets with the bounty of other continents, like glorious guacamole and avocado toast.

Monks were summoned to meals at the refectory by the sound of bells like this one, which says, "I ring for breakfast, drinks, and dinner."
Refectory bell, 13th century
The Met Cloisters, New York

Medicate Like a Monk

*It is fitting that at God's dispensation, man, who is
formed of earth, should receive relief of his infirmity from
the earth. For the earth brings forth nothing without
cause, but all by necessity.*

—The Lorsch Leechbook

It goes without saying that medicine in the Middle
Ages was definitely not as advanced as it is today. Modern technology has allowed for amazing treatments that
would have astounded medieval healers, especially the
wonder drugs that are still saving lives from the Black
Death in the hot spots where it lives today (like Arizona
and India): antibiotics. But the truth is, we wouldn't be
where we are without the medical knowledge of the medieval world, and that includes its herb lore.

If you love reading mystery novels set in the Middle
Ages, chances are you've already come across a monastic
medicinal garden, whether it was used as a source of healing or a source of poison. As we know, pretty much anything can be poisonous at the right dosage, and there were
plants to be found in medicinal gardens that could be
deadly, including nightshade and of course monkshood.
Plants like nightshade and opium poppy were used with
care to help in dire medical situations, for example am-
putations, when it was necessary to put a patient to sleep
temporarily (not permanently). Most medicinal herbs,
however, were far more benign.

Several of the plants that medieval people used for healing purposes are still used today in holistic health practices, and they are still effective. Mint, for example, noted
in medieval medical books as being useful for headaches,
is a common folk remedy used for headaches in the mod-

ern world, usually in the form of peppermint oil.[9] Fennel, said in the Middle Ages to be "useful for many medicines, but…especially applied to eye complaints," contains a chemical still used in modern medicines for conjunctivitis (pink eye). Chamomile is still used to soothe, and aloe to treat injuries to the skin.[10] Ginger, usually imported instead of homegrown, was and is used to settle the stomach. White willow bark, containing salicylic acid (the natural ingredient that is replicated in aspirin in the form of acetylsalicylic acid), was administered for pain. Mulberry, in addition to being a spiritually significant plant, as we saw earlier, was used in the treatment of burns, something that also seems to be borne out by science.[11]

The infirmarian at Barnwell Priory was expected to keep a range of herbal remedies on hand in a sort of monastic medicine cabinet to deal with the most common complaints:

> It should rarely or never happen that [the infirmarian] has not ginger, cinnamon, peony, and the like, ready in his cupboard, so as to be able to render prompt assistance to the sick if stricken by a sudden malady.[12]

With so many brothers under his care, it made sense for the infirmarian to have preparations made in advance and stored up, rather than having to take a lantern out into the garden in the middle of the night to find what he needed.

It's extremely inadvisable to start tinkering with herbal remedies on our own, as medieval people had extensive botanical knowledge that we are only just beginning to relearn. Like modern pharmacists, medieval apothecaries underwent training and apprenticeships that lasted many years before they started dispensing cures, and it's to apothecaries monks would turn if they needed any complex or dangerous medicines. The best course of action to live like a monk without accidentally poisoning ourselves is to rely on those folk medicines that are already proven by science as well as by grandmothers all over the world: warm vegetable or chicken soup, honey, and lemon for colds; ginger for upset stomach; acetylsalicylic acid for headache; and a hot cup of chamomile tea to soothe you before bed.

Rest Your Bones

Keep the prospect of death before your eyes every day.
—Benedict of Nursia, *The Rule of Saint Benedict*

A huge focus of monastic life was not life but death. The whole point of a person's earthly existence, to a monk's way of thinking, was to live well in order to achieve salvation in the afterlife. At all times, as Saint Benedict advised, a monk was to contemplate his own death and maintain a healthy fear of the divine judgment that awaited.

Medieval Christians were often directed to be mindful of their mortality and to prepare their souls for the divine judgment that awaited them. Skulls like these served as memento mori, visual reminders of death.

The Aussem Hours, fol. 66v, early 16th century (detail)
Walters Art Museum, Baltimore; W.437

Orchards not only provided food for the monastic community but were also a peaceful place to lay the dead to rest.
Ruralia commoda, fol. 28r, c. 1478–80 (detail)
British Library, London; Royal 14 E VI

Despite the impressive general knowledge of the medicinal uses of herbs that we scratched the surface of a moment ago, death was always closer in the medieval world because of poorer nutrition and a lack of antibiotics, which made every small accident that much more dangerous. Cemeteries, then, were not a rare sight, nor were they such taboo places as they are today. Often, they were places for people to gather for secular activities like games or even clandestine romantic rendezvous. In fact, in what was partially an effort to conserve space behind walls, monks were sometimes buried in the abbey orchard. Though it may make modern people squeamish,

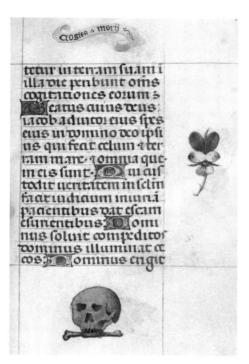

*Memento mori often appear alongside images of beauty
and life, as in this book of hours. The scroll at the top says*
Cogita morii, *"think about death."*
Book of hours, fol. 165r, c. 1500 (detail)
Walters Art Museum, Baltimore; W.427

this meant, of course, that the monk became a nourishing
part of the monastic life cycle, even in death.

For a medieval monk, the idea of returning to earth was
primarily meant to inspire feelings of humility, as no one
who was eventually going to be food for worms in the end
could be that important. As Saint Peter Damian, a Benedictine monk and cardinal of the eleventh century, put it
so colorfully,

> Come, now, brother, what is this body which you
> clothe which such diligent care and nourish gently as
> if it were royal offspring? Is it not a mass of putrefac-

tion, is it not worms, dust, and ashes? It is fit that the wise man consider not this which now is, but rather what it will be afterwards in the future....What thanks will the worms render to you, who are about to devour the flesh you nourished so tenderly and gently?[13]

This type of grotesque emphasis on the body's frailties was always a theme for Christian meditation, but never more so than after the Black Death in the fourteenth century, when people's fears about sudden and unexpected death were painfully brought to the fore. This gave rise to many memento mori ("remember death") works of art depicting people's bodies being consumed by worms and toads.

The most saintly members of the community might be embalmed and entombed within the church itself, but those supernaturally worthy people were not expected to fall into decay anyway, as many medieval saints' biographies note a pleasant smell or a lack of decomposition whenever their tombs are opened. Some of these sweet-smelling saints were Saint Oswald, Saint Thomas Becket, and even the saintly English king Henry VI.[14]

Morbid as it may sound, considering our final resting places in terms of environmental benefits in "green burials" is something that more and more modern people are embracing. Whether it's cremation, using a biodegradable coffin, or even being buried at the root of a tree, people in the modern world are thinking about the ways in which they, too, can contribute to the life cycle in death.[15] Beyond such practical considerations, modern life is likewise still full of memento mori, with memes reminding us that life is fleeting and fragile, and trends like #yolo (you only live once) encouraging us to make the most of our lives while we can.

*Memento mori were not confined to images or
manuscripts but also appeared in wall paintings, tombs,
and objects like these rosary beads, which show a tonsured
figure (rosary terminals), as he is now and as he will be
after death.*
Rosary, c. 1500–1525
The Metropolitan Museum of Art, New York

An ordinary monk spent his life in contemplation of his
own death, allowing the hope of salvation and fear of
God's judgment to guide his behavior and lead him down
a moral path. When the moment came, he expected no
more than was his due as a humble child of God: a return
to the soil that not only had once held Eden and rested
under the feet of Jesus, but that had also nourished the
monk, healed him, and provided him with spiritual comfort throughout his time on earth. As modern people,
we can follow this example in remembering the fragil-
ity of life and using the plants around us to nourish us,
body and soul, while we live, returning to the earth we
came from with humility and gratitude at the end of our
time here.

II
EMBRACE
MINIMALISM

This is true religion—that every one, according to his station, should borrow from this frail world as little as possible of food, clothes, goods, and all worldly things.
—The Ancren Riwle

In the past two decades, there has been a popular movement to embrace minimalism: the idea that we can all get along with less. The concept of not needing—or more importantly, not *wanting*—earthly things is a cornerstone of the monastic ideal. For medieval monks, the material world was fallen, sinful. From it stemmed all the temptations that pulled people away from God, and so the less involvement a person had with the physical world, the better. Early Christian hermits, from whose ascetic existence the idea of monasteries

began, took this to the extreme, living on top of stalag-
mites or wearing minimal clothing. Ordinary monks understood that this type of living was not for everyone, just
as most modern people accept that they wouldn't feel
completely happy living all their lives in a tent. Still, the
monastic lifestyle determinedly embraced minimalism in
many forms that we can learn from today.

Shrink Your Clothes

> It will suffice for a monk to have two tunics and two
> cowls, because of the need to use them at night and
> to wash them; anything more is superfluous and
> should be eliminated.
>   —Benedict of Nursia, *The Rule of Saint Benedict*

For monks, as for modern minimalists, an excess of
material possessions clutters the mind as well as
the living space, making it extremely difficult to focus
on what's important. In the abbey, of course, this meant
contemplating the divine. For the modern person, it can
mean we lose focus on the things most important in our
lives: family, friends, community, faith, wellness, or perhaps achievement.

Monks who collected objects were in danger of succumbing to greed and pride, especially, two of the cardinal
sins. When a man entered the monastery, he was to give
up his material possessions and to sign over everything
he owned to the abbey, to be disposed of as the abbot saw
fit. For people who came from a wealthy background, it
may have been difficult indeed to let go of possessions
that had been dearly bought, were valuable, or had sen-
timental value. We know that some definitely struggled
with this, stashing personal treasures and even pets like

Although the dog in this picture more likely refers to his legend than Saint Bernard's love of pets, sometimes monks and nuns did sneak pets into the cloister, including dogs, cats, and even monkeys.

Breviary of Queen Isabella of Castile, fol. 441r, c. 1497 (detail)
British Library, London; Additional 18851

cats, rabbits, or (perhaps surprisingly) monkeys.[1] But letting go of objects was part of a monk's journey, and he was expected to give up all his goods without fuss.

In fact, unlike the jubilant guests on today's reality shows who tearfully express their happiness, relief, and pride at managing to divest themselves of their clutter, medieval monks were not permitted to allow themselves to feel pride or boast about how much they'd given up. Even the poor were not permitted to rejoice that they now had clothes to wear or food to eat. According to *The Rule of Saint Augustine*,

> Let them not…imagine themselves fortunate, because they have found food and raiment such as they were unable to find abroad…but let them lift up their hearts, and seek not vain things of the earth, for fear monasteries should begin to be of use to the rich and not to the poor, if the rich are humbled therein, and the poor are puffed up.[2]

Gratitude should be expressed to God, and then the monk who has done so should move on. In this, perhaps, we shouldn't imitate medieval monks, since expressing the wide range of complex and very real emotions that can

Monks were distinguishable not just by their tonsures but also by their plain, homespun robes, much different from the brightly dyed clothes of the rest of the population.
The Abingdon Apocalypse, fol. 70r, late 13th century (detail)
British Library, London; Additional 42555

come from divesting ourselves of extra stuff—even when we don't need or want it anymore—is probably better for our mental health. (Monks did struggle with their mental health at times, a topic we'll look at in chapter three.)

All property that belonged to the monastery was meant to be communal, even down to the clothing that monks wore. In reality, monks were permitted their own clothes (for practical reasons like size), and some monasteries were known to have had each monk's name stitched on the inside of his robes so that the clothing didn't get mixed up when it went through the laundry or to the tailor.[3] Saint Benedict envisioned a storeroom of clothes of slightly better quality than everyday wear, which monks could borrow for journeys—a brotherly closet which included communal underwear meant to be washed and put back.[4] It's not clear just how widespread the communal undies idea extended beyond Saint Benedict's own monastery at Montecassino, but this is one case in which you definitely *shouldn't* try to live like a monk.

In terms of clothes, Saint Benedict decreed that in addition to their two tunics and cowls, monks could also have a winter cowl and a summer one and "a scapular for work."[5] Sticking to this rule to the letter was difficult at times; one Scottish abbey actually had to petition the

Cistercian monks followed The Rule of Saint Benedict *to the letter and wore white, undyed robes to show their pious disdain for fashion.*
Psalter, c. 1501–2 (detail)
The Metropolitan Museum of Art, New York

pope for permission to wear woolen hats in church, since they were freezing in winter.[6]

Doubtless, we can all agree that we probably need more than just two sets of daily clothes and one pair of shoes, and that our underwear, especially, should be ours alone. A monastic minimum standard, however, definitely puts our own closets into perspective. Organizational professionals recommend we tackle our wardrobes as a beginning step to making more space in our lives for the important things.[7] Donating our gently used clothing to the needy is one way in which we can follow the monastic example if we choose to shrink the contents of our closets.

When it comes to other material objects, the list of what a monk should keep with him is predictably short. According to Saint Benedict, the abbot should supply "everything necessary" to each brother, which (in addition to "a mat, blanket, cover, and pillow") included: "cowl, tunic, leggings, boots, belt, knife, stylus, needle, handkerchief, and [wax] tablets."[8] In a nutshell, a monk should need only bedding, clothes, something to eat with, something to write with, something to make repairs with, and something to keep him from wiping his nose on the sleeve he needs to wear several days in a row. Fair enough.

For a modern person, it's worth taking note of the

Because parchment was expensive and labor-intensive to create, quick notes could be scratched into the wax contained in tablets like this. Wax tablets were one of the few possessions each monk was permitted, according to The Rule of Saint Benedict. Writing tablet, c. 14th century The Met Cloisters, New York

things that we surround ourselves with, and considering whether or not we actually need them, or if we just want them. Many of the things we need can, as was the case with medieval monks, be shared or borrowed through friends, communal stores, and libraries, so we must consider the question of what we really need to make our lives comfortable and meaningful, and what we might be wasting our money on (the next way in which we can learn from our frugal brothers).

While it's true that most of us probably have many more material possessions than we need, rare is the person who can happily live out of a backpack for more than a few weeks or months, and even monks had to be called to the carpet sometimes to hand over the treasures they'd stored. When it comes to the things we surround ourselves with as modern people, it's far healthier for us to find our own personal happy medium between too much and too little. Medieval monks could expect to receive new shoes every year, at which point they'd donate their old ones. This is a handy goal for our own lives too: an annual spring cleaning of our wardrobe and possessions with anything extra going to charity, is a noble—and manageable—aim for us all.

Change How You Spend Your Change

*First, cast out money, for Christ and money do not
go well together in one place.... If money is there,
let it retire forthwith into other halls so that Christ
may find vacant the cell of your heart.*
                                          —Saint Peter Damian

Something both we, as modern people, and medieval monks can agree on is that owning a lot of material possessions means a person has been spending a large
chunk of change on himself. To the monastic mind, this
was a problem in part because of the dangers it posed to
the spender's soul: he was focusing too much on earthly
comfort instead of spiritual comfort, putting himself at
risk of succumbing to greed and pride, as we saw. It also
meant that this was money that could have been spent on
charitable causes instead of sinful ones.

The medieval monastery wasn't just a place for monks
to live and pray. It was also an important part of the
greater community as a place of refuge and respite. Travelers were always welcome at a monastery, bound as the
brothers were to treat every stranger as if he were Jesus
come again. This humble welcome extended as far as the
expectations that monks bow or prostrate themselves before guests, and for the abbot himself to wash their hands
and even their feet.[9] As monasteries were usually established on the outskirts of cities in order to provide more
privacy, quiet, and solitude for the monks, they were convenient stopping places for travelers, especially those who
wanted to save themselves the cost of a stay at an inn. Donations from visitors were very welcome and indeed expected. The notorious King John of England made it

into the *Chronicle of the Abbey of Bury St Edmunds* for his stinginess:

> King John, ignoring all his other commitments, came to St. Edmund's immediately after his coronation, impelled by a vow and out of devotion. We naturally thought that he would make a sizeable donation, but he gave only a silk cloth which his servants had on loan from our sacrist—and still they have not paid for it. Although he had accepted St. Edmund's most generous hospitality, when he left he contributed nothing at all honourable or beneficial to the Saint, except the 13s. which he gave at Mass on the day he left us.[10]

Even in the Middle Ages, people remembered bad tippers.

Because monasteries frequently were the guardians of sacred relics, they could expect regular visits from

Relics like the bones of saints were thought to have spiritual powers and were kept safe in reliquaries often shaped like the body part they contained, such as this one, made to contain the skull of the sixth-century French abbot Saint Yrieix (Aredius).
Reliquary bust of Saint Yrieix, c. 1220–40
The Metropolitan Museum of Art, New York

Pilgrims often visited monastic shrines to pray for help or ask forgiveness, collecting badges like this one as devotional objects or status symbols.
Pilgrim's badge, c. 14th century
The Met Cloisters, New York

pilgrims, like John, who were seeking saints' help or venerating them. Saints were believed to have many different powers, including capabilities to heal, increase fertility, bring success to business endeavors, and intercede on behalf of a sinner. Many medieval monasteries were dedicated to local saints, whose miracles were concentrated there.

Monasteries encouraged the veneration of their own saints by recording their miracles, thereby spreading the saints' reputations farther afield. Stories of these miracles brought pilgrim traffic, an essential part of monastic funding. Pilgrims could buy badges as a souvenir of their journey or as a focus for devotion, and their donations of money to have Masses said for themselves or their loved ones allowed monks to plow the money back into the monasteries, shoring up areas of disrepair, building new additions, or embellishing their church with the type of decoration that would both make it a worthy place to worship God and meet pilgrims' expectations of what a house of God should look like.

Despite the flow of cash coming in from donations and landholdings, sometimes monasteries struggled financially, since monks, being human, were occasionally reluctant to give up the power that comes with currency. This led to moments like one at Bury Saint Edmunds when the monks were called to the chapter house and compelled to relinquish any personal seals they had secreted away—these were, effectively, their signatures to guarantee the repayment of debts taken on, sometimes in the name of the abbey itself. "When this was done," says the chronicler Jocelin of Brakelond, "the total was found to be thirty-three seals," an astonishingly high number.[11] When Abbot Samson (who we'll meet in chapter four) took this overspending in hand, he was able to use the money to better administer the abbey and undertake a number of essential building projects. Although a flawed individual himself, the abbot knew that while medieval buildings like cathedrals often take years, even generations, to complete, the end result is something that brings joy to both the builders and to the community.

It's much more fun to use our personal seals to finance luxuries, but we know deep down that borrowing money against the future for our present satisfaction can lead to uncomfortable situations. Spending money on necessities that allow us to do good work, for ourselves and for others, is the better path. The abbots who looked to the long term, investing in spaces and technologies that would allow the monastery to thrive, are the ones who are remembered kindly by history.

While it's not necessary to cut all spending in the way of a medieval monk—moderation, as we'll see in this book's final chapter, is key—we know that every penny we save grows over time, just as every wise investment, whether it's in education, a home, or helpful technology, pays off in the end. It may be difficult, and even embarrassing, to take ourselves to the chapter house and face our spending habits, but the things we build with discipline around money will pay dividends in the future.

Make Space for Yourself

When we asked the Lord about who lived in his dwell-
ing place, we heard his teaching about living there,
but it is up to us to fulfill the dweller's duties.
    —Benedict of Nursia, *The Rule of Saint Benedict*

P erhaps one of the most eye-catching trends of modern minimalism is the move toward tiny houses.
Homes with a footprint of only a few hundred square feet
boast a small carbon footprint as well—something medieval monks would have approved of, given their dedication
to reusing and recycling the gifts of nature with an eye toward long-term sustainability. Monks would also have approved of the intentional use of only a small space; after
all, ideally they would have spent all their time in prayer.
A familiar figure in some medieval towns who lived this
way on a permanent basis was the anchorite, a person
who took monastic ideals back to their eremitic extremes
by enclosing himself or herself within a room or two for
life, continuously engaged in spiritual contemplation.
Anchorites, however, relied on the community to provide
food for them, something that a tiny-home owner isn't
likely to be able to do (barring an endless flow of restau-
rant delivery). While space is sacrificed in modern tiny
homes, comfort isn't; tiny homes contain all the luxuries
of modern living, including entertainment and technology meant to make life easy. For the medieval monk, and
especially for an anchorite, making life easy was missing
the point entirely.

    Beyond shrinking living spaces, modern minimalism
seems to be defined, in a visual sense, to white space, un-
cluttered by a lot of art or patterned wallpaper. While a
monk's own cell might well be plain, monastic minimal-

Monastic ideals of minimalism didn't extend to devotional objects or those used for the Mass, like this chalice. Its intricacy was meant to elevate the chalice and make it worthy to contain the wine that was to transform into the blood of Jesus.
Chalice, c. 1230–50
The Met Cloisters, New York

ism didn't extend to decoration. Medieval cloisters and churches were filled with color, from the patterned floor tiles to the stained glass windows. Rich cloth adorned altars, ornate chalices were used for Mass, and stonework was routinely carved with everything from curling leaves to grinning gargoyles. While monks believed that adorning the self was sinful and would lead to excessive pride, this attitude did not extend to their buildings, whose purpose was to glorify God and to be a testament to the ardent devotion of the monks. The elaborate Gothic style of architecture and decoration was devotional and became a hallmark of the medieval style of worship, looked down upon by the followers of a new kind of faith in the centuries following the Middle Ages: Protestantism. Enthusiastic decorating wasn't just for show, however.

One of the trendiest trends in self-help at the moment is creating a "vision board": a sort of scrapbook for the wall of all the things a person wants to gain or accomplish in life. Vision boards are meant to encompass everything

Brilliant illumination allowed brothers to express their love of color and their love of God.
Omne Bonum (Absolucio-Circumcisio), fol. 16r, c. 1360–75
British Library, London; Royal 6 E VI

from the patio set of our dreams to our ideal vacation or career. Modern science has shown that goal setting is important and visualizing success even more so when it comes to achieving outcomes. This is seen most prominently during the Olympics, when gold medalists are interviewed after their wins. Among the many components of success, including mentorship, dedication, and natural talent, is visualizing not only the win itself but also the perfect performance that led up to it. Repetition of this visualization allows athletes to believe in the possibility of their vision becoming a dream that literally comes true, a self-fulfilling prophecy.

For medieval monks, the walls of the church were a sort of vision board, too, that gave focus to the goals of the brothers. Illustrations of saints and angels, heaven and hell, the suffering of Jesus, and the serenity of Mary showed them not only the path to salvation, and the pitfalls along the way, but the divine blessings that awaited them. Every time the brothers entered the church, they were reminded of the heavenly reward they could achieve, allowing them to focus on the goal and keeping them motivated to attain it.

To live like a monk, then, is to have a home that is efficient in its purpose, where we are surrounded by those things that help us to live the lifestyle we want and keep us motivated to achieve our goals. However we choose to decorate, whether it's in the solid white of modern minimalism or the riotous color of the medieval church, our homes and spaces should lift the spirit and encourage us to be the people we wish to be as we move through our everyday routines.

Build Your Community with Purpose

> Since no one has the capacity to receive all spiritual gifts, but the grace of the Spirit is given proportionately to the faith of each, when one is living in association with others, the grace privately bestowed on each individual becomes the common possession of his fellows.
> —Saint Basil, *The Long Rules*

One of the other places modern organizational experts discuss simplifying our lives is, of course, in the realm of social media. Our modern social circles have become enormous, sometimes including hundreds—if not thousands—of "friends." In person, we likely have only a few dozen close friends, while the rest are acquaintances. In the past, these were people who would fall by the wayside, and who we'd see only at scheduled reunions, unless we made an active effort to keep in touch. Because of social media, people who we haven't seen since kindergarten and who live across continents and oceans can now be privy to the smallest details of our lives, including photos of the food we eat.

While modern privacy experts find our widespread oversharing appalling, medieval monks would be flabbergasted, not by the fact that we're sharing our lunches—although that would definitely flummox them, as it does so many of us—but by the sheer scale of our everyday social networks.

Most medieval monks lived in communities with only a few dozen people, although the more popular ones housed a few hundred. This might seem like a lot, but two or even three hundred people is fewer than the student body of an average Western high school, and we all know how many differing social relationships can be born and fostered there. No doubt monks would have known every other member of their communities, even if only in passing. The number of people they were in contact with beyond the walls varied considerably, with the abbot continuing to foster relationships with tenants and members of the greater community, including the nobility, for the purpose of administering the monastery and its landholdings. Other monks might have contact with people from the town and the countryside for things like buying and selling crafts and food or working in an attached or affiliated hospital. Although they obviously would not have forgotten the families, friends, or communities they came from before they joined the monastery, monks were not encouraged to keep up ties. Outsiders were a distraction: that's the very reason the monastery had walls.

It wasn't always an easy task for monks to leave behind the lives they knew. Monks like the eleventh- to twelfth-century historian Orderic Vitalis, an oblate from England who was sent to France and remained there for life, sometimes spoke wistfully of their past lives and homes. Occasionally, monks kept in touch with family members; however, any letters received were read by monks higher up the chain, and any care packages were distributed throughout the community, according to need. As Saint Benedict explained:

> In no way should it be allowed for a monk to receive letters, gifts, or keepsakes, not from his relatives, any other person, or another monk, nor should he give them, without the abbot's permission. But if something has been sent to him by his relatives, he should not presume to receive it unless the abbot is informed beforehand. But if the abbot orders it to be received, it should be in his power to command to whom it should be given and the brother to whom it happened to have been sent should not be upset, lest "the Devil be given an opportunity."[12]

Those warm wool socks a monk's mother made him, then, could easily have ended up on the feet of the elderly Brother William instead of his own. This didn't make for much motivation to keep up ties.

Like high schoolers, or people on airplanes, or any other group that spends an extended amount of time together, monks created friendships and relationships with the people they saw on a daily basis. As with any group that shares experiences—especially difficult or challenging ones—these were the people who could understand the monk's life, as no one else could—the hardship, the routine, Brother John's snoring, and everything in between.

For monks, the synergy of shared experience and com-

*When monks took vows, their communities shrunk down to
a handful of people who held the same values, performed the
same duties, and shared the same trials.*
Book of hours, fol. 166v, c. 1430–35 (detail)
Walters Art Museum, Baltimore; W.168

mon purpose was essential to making the monastery run
smoothly. Novices had a yearlong probationary period for
the sole purpose of ensuring the right fit for both themselves and for the community. As the author of Barnwell Priory's *Observances* remarked, "Brethren should be
careful not to choose those of whose election they may

afterwards repent."[13] As we've seen, the whole point of establishing monasteries in the first place was to have the
faithful work together to help each other avoid sin and
achieve salvation, so it was essential that the relationships
within the monastic community were solid. The inter-
ference of people who did not share the same outlook or
goals was an unwelcome disruption.

The major difference between relationships in the modern world and those in the monastic world is that geogra-
phy is no longer a factor. Once a monk had entered monastic
life, his old life fell away. For modern people, when we grad-
uate from school, move towns, or change jobs, that need
not be the end of our relationships; in fact, people are now
expected and even pressured to keep in touch. For a monk,
this clinging to the past would be unnecessary in many
ways and irrelevant to the life he was now living.

A popular maxim is that we are the average of our five
closest relationships; we fall in the middle of these people
in terms of happiness, education, and even weight.
Whether or not this is true in literal terms, science has
shown that we are incredibly influenced by the actions
of our peers, such that when a member of our peer group
becomes more physically active or gets divorced, we are
more likely to as well. This also holds true for success: if
the people we surround ourselves with are successful, we
will be too.[14]

If this is the case (and it is), it's worth looking into our
relationships and seeing whether the people we're spending the most time with are enriching our lives or detract-
ing from them. The advantage of the vast network of our
relationships, through social media especially, is that it
gives us opportunities to build our communities thoughtfully, allowing us to join like-minded groups and build or
solidify relationships with people who can support and
mentor us and who we can support in return. The synergy

of a monastic house is something we can use as a model: our relationships can and should be mutually beneficial to our friends, our greater community, and ourselves.

Embrace Silence

> *Want of control of the tongue is an evident sign of a dissolute mind and of a neglected conscience.*
> —*Observances* of Barnwell Priory

Beyond clinging to relationships with people outside of our current sphere or phase of life, what would have horrified monastic thinkers like Saint Benedict would have been the massive amount of chatter modern people participate in on a daily basis. Monks were meant to be silent for most of the day, barring services or if they had something important to say in chapter. While they were permitted to talk at certain times, like the brothers of Barnwell Priory, who could speak if they needed to between none and vespers, the ultimate goal was always silence. At Barnwell, even during free time, no one was allowed to speak unless the most senior brother present started the conversation by saying "Benedicite" (giving a blessing).

Saint Benedict believed that mindless chatter was at best distracting and at worst destructive. This is why he insisted on silence at mealtimes, except for the solitary voice of the monk who was assigned to read to the brothers that week from an edifying text. Saint Benedict's major fear around speech was that brothers might question or voice skepticism about the abbey's core beliefs or practices, leading to spreading doubt and dissent throughout the community. If a brother had a question about the text being read at dinner, or the decisions made by the abbot, he was not to voice this aloud in front of other brothers but take it to a senior monk later.[15]

Although the goal was always silence, occasionally brothers were permitted to talk together, preferably about holy topics.
Decretum, fol. 210v, late 13th–early 14th century (detail)
British Library, London; Royal 11 D IX

Silence presented some challenges, in that sometimes it actually *is* necessary to communicate when you need something. For that reason, hungry monks came up with a rudimentary sign language to get them the things they needed without interrupting the reading. Signs like "pass the salt" were written down in books so that they could be shared with other monasteries to make life a little easier for everyone. An Old English copy of the *Monasteriales Indicia* contains 127 signs for monks to use for everyday items or tasks. Some of these signs would still be understood today—for example, rubbing your hands together to ask someone to pass you the soap. However, other signs, like stroking your hands up your thighs to ask someone to pass you your underwear, would probably lead to some misunderstandings.[16]

Of course, anyone who's tried to be serious during a long church service, school day, or boring meeting at work knows that we don't need to speak to communicate. A raised eyebrow, a sigh, or—heaven forbid—a stifled giggle can be enough to derail a serious moment, without a single word spoken. Saint Benedict no doubt had seen this too often for himself when he wrote,

> As soon as the signal for the divine office is heard, the
> brothers, leaving behind whatever is in their hands,
> should hasten with all speed, yet seriously, without
> sparking frivolity.[17]

While it's easy to spark frivolity by quietly racing your
brothers to church, and to express boredom or frustration
through body language alone, sharing your every random
thought about your lunch, your favorite podcast, or your
musings on reality television is nearly impossible without
some sort of speech. Saint Benedict's insistence on silence
effectively cut down on silliness and gossip, although evi-
dently not entirely. *The Ancren Riwle*, a thirteenth-century
guide for anchorites, laments the common saying "from
miln and from market, from smithy and from nunnery,
men bring tidings."[18]

What Saint Benedict realized, and what led to his frequent admonitions against grumbling in his *Rule*, was
that words shape our reality. Through the words we tell
ourselves and each other, we form narratives about ourselves and the world, which in turn influence how we
perceive it and how we function within it. Saint Benedict
feared that much grumbling about the hardship of monastic life would make the whole project untenable, as
the brothers would believe such austerity was impossible. He even went so far as to say, "We caution this, above
all: brothers should refrain from grumbling."[19] Insisting
on a silence filled only by the words of the church fathers,
scripture, and prayer instead was a way to continuously
frame the brothers' perception of their reality and their
journey as positive and worthwhile.

Scientific study has shown that this is still the case
for people in the modern world. Those who spend their
time absorbing pessimistic talk through other people or
through media view the world more negatively, while

reframing adversity in positive terms is the best way to weather emotional storms. Some of these studies have been done involving people who live in austere environments, like the poles or space.[20]

Instead of filling our ears with mindless chatter, it's important that we consciously decide who and what we listen to, so that we can focus on a narrative framework that expresses the way we prefer our lives to be. This may involve journaling, conversation with a supportive person, or positive affirmations.[21] Repeating words of comfort, hope, and faith can bolster us and help us cope with life's difficulties, just as it did for medieval monks.

Supercharge Your Habits

We are incapable by nature of following success-
fully a number of pursuits at the same time; to fin-
ish one task with diligent care is more beneficial
than to undertake many and not complete them.
                —Saint Basil, *The Long Rules*

Everyone from ancient philosophers to modern productivity gurus tells us that forming good habits is a surefire way to leading a life that is less stressful, more productive, and more meaningful. If anyone can demonstrate the fact that our habits become who we are, it's medieval monks and nuns. After all, it's not a coincidence that the uniform still worn by nuns, based on modest medieval clothes, is called a habit.

One of the key ways habits can make us more productive, say modern experts, is that they streamline our lives by removing the necessity for decision-making.[22] When we spend less time weighing options about small things, we have more time for the things we actually want to spend our time on. For Saint Benedict, this was one of

A nun's outfit, based on simple medieval clothes, is still called a "habit."

Book of hours (use of Liège), fol. 93r, c. 1300–1310 (detail) Walters Art Museum, Baltimore; W.37

the main goals of writing down his *Rule* in the first place. He was not only trying to establish what he thought was the best system for the running of an orderly and suitably worshipful monastic house, but he was also removing any need for guesswork on the part of the monks. If you needed an answer, you could just refer to the *Rule*.[23]

Over and above the *Rule* itself was the monks' obligation to obey the abbot in all things. Obedience was one of the three major vows a monk made upon his induction into the community, and its importance is repeatedly stressed by Saint Benedict, who declares, "Whoever, renounce[es] his own will in order to fight for the Lord Christ, the true king, takes up the brilliant and mighty weapons of obedience."[24] Even if the monk believed in his heart that the abbot was wrong, he was to offer that worry up to God and obey.

In practice, people being people, abbots were not obeyed in all things. We know that brothers did things like sneaking personal items into the abbey and meeting lovers in the orchard. In a similar way, what we know about ourselves as modern people is that we are just as apt to neglect our vows, as our strings of unmet New Year's resolutions can attest. But medieval monks can teach us yet another way to create—and stick to—the habits we want to keep: establishing rituals.

Rituals are supercharged habits—habits imbued with meaning. For medieval monks, naturally, the meaning behind each ritual was always spiritual. The ritual of the Eucharist recalled the Last Supper, during which Jesus told his disciples that the bread and wine they were about to eat represented his body and blood given in sacrifice; the ritual of washing another's feet recalled Jesus, Martha, and the apostles of the New Testament doing the same, in humility and without regard for their own health; the ritual of ringing the bells invoked celebration, gathering, and urgency. The monastic day was completely filled with ritualized activity that was both spiritual and practical. When the brothers washed their hands before eating, they were reminded of spiritual cleansing, while also cleansing their bodies. When they woke at the same time each day to celebrate matins, they were beginning the work of their days, but also setting their circadian rhythms. When they greeted and blessed each other as they passed, they were remembering the blessings of their spiritual mentors and also building relationships.

For modern people with less of a focus on spirituality, the second part of these rituals might be the goal instead— good hygiene, a healthy sleep routine, and fulfilling rela- tionships—but the end result is the same. When we want to build a habit that will make our lives better, the best way to do it is to give it meaning beyond the activity itself, meaning that connects us to the people we want to be. In- vesting in habits that reinforce our identities allows us to keep them going, even on days when we're tempted to quit. For medieval brothers, identifying as a monk, a ser-

The monastic routine was ruled by the sound of bells,
which called the brothers to wakefulness, to meals, and
to prayer.
Omne Bonum (Absolucio-Circumcisio), fol. 232, c. 1360–75 (detail)
British Library, London; Royal 6 E VI

vant of Jesus, was fundamental to their sense of self, making their rituals ones that they could stick to, and come back to easily, even if they slipped up.[25]

One last way that we can look to medieval monks to supercharge our habits and streamline our lives is by emulating the structured routine of their days. The monastic routine was based on the calendar year and the canonical hours, both of which told the monks when and what to pray, read, and sing. Each day, they knew they'd have a service, then a break, then another activity, then a service, and so on.

A popular method of increasing productivity these days is based on the HIIT (high intensity interval training) strategy of physical training. The idea is that people complete their tasks in "sprints"; they set a timer, work for that whole time without distraction, and then reward them-selves with a break or a different activity. The reasoning behind this is that it is a whole lot easier to concentrate on something for a short stretch, especially if you know you have a reward coming.

Perhaps to the dismay of modern productivity experts, the medieval monastic lifestyle had already figured out the usefulness of this system. Not only did the monks have scheduled times to work and pray, but they also had scheduled breaks—meal breaks, leisure, and even bath-room breaks. As Saint Benedict delicately puts it, "The schedule should be regulated so that, [matins] complete, there is a very brief break during which the brothers may go out for the necessities of nature."[26]

To be fair, medieval monks had the advantage of not having smartphones connecting them to an entire world of people and information 24/7, so perhaps focus-ing on a single task for an extended period of time was slightly easier for them. That said, we are not slaves to our smartphones—no matter how much we may *feel* like it at times—and if we wish to gain the dedicated focus of me-dieval monks, it's worth our while to pay attention to how they accomplished it.

The core tenet of minimalism is to reduce distractions so that we can focus on what's important to us, and for the same reason, minimalism was a fundamental compo-nent of medieval monastic life. While it's true that there were fewer distractions in the medieval world in the form of notifications and demands on our time, we are still the ones who control both the amount of stimulation we take in and the activities we fill our time with. If we can mini-mize our possessions, fill our lives with real and fulfilling relationships, and supercharge our habits, we can find the space we need to move on to the next part of monastic liv-ing: inner peace.

Seek peace and pursue it.
—Benedict of Nursia, *The Rule of Saint Benedict*

long with minimalism, one of the trendiest movements today is "mindfulness," a word that appears everywhere from online advertisements for lush yoga retreats to corporate memos to bold font in the checkout line. For modern people, run off our feet and constantly bombarded with noise, news, and chatter, mindfulness offers a way to slow down and tune into ourselves—our values, our needs, and our goals. For a medieval monk, mindfulness was being aware of himself and his own place in the universe. Taking lessons in mindfulness from a medieval monk is a good way to reconnect with ourselves as individuals and as interconnected beings.

Meditate

> Forget…all the world, and there be intirely [sic] out of the body; there in glowing love embrace your beloved [Savior] who is come down from heaven into your breast's bower, and hold him fast until he shall have granted whatever you wish for.
>
> —The Ancren Riwle

Meditation is thousands of years old, extending well before the medieval era and, doubtless, well into the future. Nowadays, meditation tends to be associated with Eastern traditions, especially Buddhism, to the point that it may seem to have no part of the Christian tradition at all. But spiritual practice in both Buddhism and Christianity involves both prayer *and* meditation.

Some people describe prayer as an active state: a person speaks to divinity, asking for advice or guidance or perhaps pouring out grief or gratitude. Meditation, on the other hand, is frequently described as much more passive: a person listens to divinity, leaving themselves open to whatever lessons, guidance, or comfort is to be imparted to them. Sitting alone and removing even the distraction of our own desires can make it easier to let ideas come to us. After all, as *The Ancren Riwle* says, "An angel has seldom appeared to man in a crowd."[1] The lines between prayer and meditation are often a little blurry, but the categories of speaking and listening are useful as guidelines.

The idea of meditation as sitting still with a blank mind is one that is pervasive today, and in the pursuit of that unattainable goal, many people give up. Instead, meditation can be focusing on one thing only (as much as possible)

Meditation is sometimes considered to be a way of quieting the mind, leaving it open for divine comfort or inspiration.
Prayer book, fol. 14r,
early 16th century (detail)
Walters Art Museum, Baltimore; W.432

and coming back to that focus when our minds inevitably wander. While modern people usually put their focus on their breathing, or on simply being aware of the present moment, our monastic brothers put their focus on spiritual themes.

In the Middle Ages, a major theme for spiritual meditation was the mortal body of Jesus, especially his suffering. This makes sense theologically, as it is the suffering of Jesus that made eternal salvation possible, but it also makes sense on a practical level, as Jesus's humanity was much more relatable than his divinity. While it's difficult to understand the vastness of the cosmos, physical pain is something all humans can relate to intimately. A deep understanding of the physical pain of the human body of Jesus was meant to lead to an understanding of the magnitude of his sacrifice.

Some of the people who delved furthest into this form of meditation were female religious, especially anchorites. Julian of Norwich, an anchorite who wrote in the fifteenth century, recorded visions of Jesus on which she would later meditate, many of which involved his blood, sweat, and tears. Her very first vision was of Jesus's crown of thorns:

*Monks were encouraged to meditate on the humanity of Jesus
in order to better understand his suffering.*
Prayer book, fol. 57v, c. 1500 (detail)
Walters Art Museum, Baltimore; W.436

Suddenly I saw the red blood trickling down from under the garland, hot and freshly, and right plentifully, as it was in the time of His passion when the garland of thorns was pressed on His blessed head.[2]

Julian's vision came to her in response to her plea that she be allowed to suffer with Jesus, but monastic meditation did not have to be gruesome. As in the earlier ex-

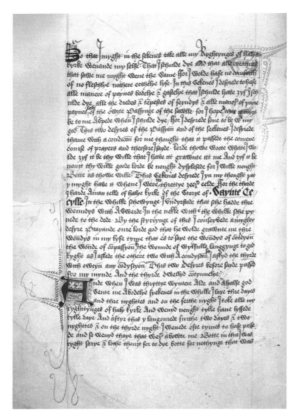

Julian of Norwich, a fifteenth-century anchorite, recorded her vivid visions of Jesus and meditations on his love after she was enclosed. This passage describes the moment Julian received her visions, at the age of thirty (and a half).

The Amherst Manuscript, fol. 97v, mid-15th century
British Library, London; Additional 37790

ample from *The Ancren Riwle*, it was perfectly acceptable, and encouraged, to sit and bask in a pleasant meditation on the love of Jesus instead. Brothers were also encouraged to meditate on the works of the saints, the faithfulness of the apostles, or the grace of Mary. One holy monk in *The Dialogue on Miracles* (a collection of Cistercian sto-

One of the most common themes for meditation, especially for women, was the suffering of the Virgin Mary at the death of her son.

The Virgin Supported by Saint John, c. 1340–50
The Metropolitan Museum of Art, New York

ries from the thirteenth century) tells a novice, "When you are at prayer, do not speak, but simply meditate upon the nativity, the passion, the Resurrection of the Saviour, and all else that you know about him."[3] Even Julian's meditations were sometimes tame, such as when she reflected on a vision in which Jesus handed her a hazelnut, and she realized that even small things like this contained the vastness of God's love.[4]

The mental and physical benefits of meditation have been and continue to be studied by modern scientists, and the results are surprising. Meditation has been shown to make people feel calmer and deal better with—or even recover from—trauma, anxiety, and depression, all of which might be expected; however, the benefits of meditative practice seem to be lasting, even for those who stop. People who meditate are better at managing their emotions for years afterward, which makes them better able

*Holy images, like this one of Jesus's wounded hand, were
believed to have power in them and were a good focus
for meditation. The dirt accumulated on the parchment
indicates that this page was used often.*
Book of hours, fol. 140v, c. 1460–70 (detail)
Walters Art Museum, Baltimore; W.202

to cope with the stresses of life in the long term. Although
many practitioners recommend twenty minutes of daily
meditation, studies have shown that people's mental
health can improve with a habit as short as three minutes.[5]

The spiritual calm that we associate with medieval
monks may have come from their assurance of their place
in the world and the certainty of eternal bliss if they lived
and died well. As it turns out, their sense of placid well-
being may also have come from an established daily meditation practice, which trained their minds to focus on the
things they felt were most important.

No matter what we choose to meditate on, provided we
are focusing on the positive or the neutral and not just ru-
minating on our problems, establishing a regular meditation habit, like a medieval monk, may bring us lasting
peace and serenity—without our having to take a vow of
chastity.

Read

Often, dear sisters, ye ought to pray less, that ye may
read more.... In reading, when the heart feels delight,
devotion ariseth, and that is worth many prayers.
                                    —*The Ancren Riwle*

Monks, especially those who arrived at the monastery as children, were given a formal education (see chapter four) for the primary purpose of teaching them to read. More than just a hobby, reading was central to monastic life, and monks were expected to spend a significant amount of time reading each day, especially on Sunday.

While it was essential for monks to know their scripture, the book of Psalms in particular, monastic libraries were filled with treasures far beyond just the Bible and *The Rule of Saint Benedict*. Holy texts included the works of the early church fathers, such as Saint Jerome and Saint Augustine, who served as examples of reformed sinners who achieved the perfection of sainthood, and who were

Monasteries housed a wide variety of books for reading, studying, and copying. Here, Roman philosopher Boethius sits among neat rows of books ready for study.
Le Livre de Boece de Consolacion, fol. 1r, 1477 (detail)
British Library, London; Harley 4335

also the theological heavyweights upon whose work much of the medieval church's ideas were built.

Other holy texts included hagiographies, or saints' lives, exciting stories that detailed the harrowing trials and martyrdoms of the saints as well as their supernatural powers. Hagiographies could be nearly as salacious as modern adventure books and television shows, as female

Saints' lives, or hagiographies, provided moral lessons as well as being juicy tales that involved miracles, violence, and even nudity, as in the story of Saint Catherine (pictured).

The Limbourg Brothers (active 1399–1416), *The Belles Heures of Jean, duc de Berry*, fol. 17v, 1405–1408/9 (detail)
The Met Cloisters, New York

saints, like Saint Catherine, tended to be stripped naked by their pagan enemies before being tortured and killed, achieving miracles along the way. In addition to the racy text, hagiographies sometimes contained pictures of the saints, which may have prompted not just spiritual inspiration but the sort of lusty thoughts for which a brother would later have to confess.

Although the early modern period is often associated with the Renaissance or "rebirth" of classical learning, medieval monks before this time were familiar with the works of ancient thinkers like Plato and Aristotle, whose ideas they integrated into Christianity in complex ways. Aristotle's ideas on natural philosophy were particularly admired, even if they seemed to contradict biblical teachings, as they shone a light on the workings of the physical world whose truths could not be ignored.

In addition to the works of the ancient philosophers, monastic libraries were stocked with books by ancient and contemporary physicians. Cassiodorus, a sixth-century abbot, makes explicit that the monks of his abbey were to read ancient medical sources:

> First of all the *Herb Book* of Dioscorides, who has treated and portrayed the herbs of the fields with remarkable accuracy. After this read Latin translations of Hippocrates and Galen....Finally, read Caelius Aurelianus's *On Medicine*, and Hippocrates's *On Herbs and Cures*, and various other works written on the art of medicine; with God's help, I have left you these books, stored away in the recesses of our library.[6]

Cassiodorus's declaration that he has built this collection for the monks with God's help shows that the wisdom of the ancient world, though pagan, was to be treasured, not despised.

Monks were individually loaned books to read at Lent and expected to treat them with care.
Beaupré Antiphonary, vol. 3, fol. 207v, c. 1280 (detail)
Walters Art Museum, Baltimore; W.761

In addition to the works of the ancients, and perhaps more surprisingly, monks collected the works of Islamic thinkers, many of whom were far ahead of Europeans in their knowledge of medicine, astronomy, physics, and mathematics. The *Canon of Medicine* by Abū-ʿAlī al-Ḥusayn ibn-ʿAbdallāh Ibn-Sīnā—known to Europeans as Avicenna—was the go-to text for medical study, while Muhammad ibn Musa al-Khwarizmi's calculus pushed Christian thinkers to new heights of mathematical discovery.[7]

Most monks were not permitted to browse the monastic library willy-nilly, however. Books were assigned based
on the knowledge that a monk was to acquire. Specifically,
at the beginning of Lent, the librarian would hand out
books to each brother for his spiritual edification. At Barnwell Priory, the librarian also kept careful track of borrow-
ers, much like his modern counterparts, "enter[ing] on
his roll the titles of the books, and the names of those who
receive them." In addition, the librarian was charged with
correcting "mistakes of the readers," dusting, repairing,
and binding the abbey's books.[8]

Reading in the Middle Ages was not normally a silent
activity, but in the cloister, a brother was meant to read
quietly enough that he did not disturb the others, not
even by turning the pages too loudly.[9] Saint Benedict
placed such an emphasis on quiet, focused reading that
his warnings for disruptive brothers were dire:

> Above all, one or two senior monks should be as-
> signed to go around the monastery during the hours
> the brothers are free for reading and see to it that
> there is no slothful brother who spends his time in
> idleness or gossip and neglects his reading; such a

*Saint Benedict (pictured) insisted
that every monk read regularly,
with punishments meted out to
those who disturbed the brothers'
concentration.*
Prayer book, fol. 21r,
early 16th century (detail)
Walters Art Museum, Baltimore; W.432

one is not only harmful to himself but also a distraction to others. If, God forbid, such a person is discovered, he should be corrected a first and second time; if he does not amend, he should be subjected to the correction of the Rule in such a way that the others are afraid.[10]

The importance of reading for monastic brethren cannot be overstated, and many modern people take a similar view. Daily reading is a practice that many high achievers credit as a big part of the secret to their success.[11] The inspirational speaker and writer Earl Nightingale famously said that studying an hour every day on one subject would make a person a world expert in a matter of years, and certainly the goal for monks was to become experts in theology—if not in preaching it, then at least in understanding it.

While the depth of a person's reading in a subject is important, and certainly leads to expertise, perhaps equally important is the breadth of our reading, as the variety of books in monastic libraries attests. Steve Jobs, one of the twentieth century's most celebrated innovators, credited the breadth of courses he audited at university as being a big part of Apple's famously unique design. Among the courses he cited as being most influential was one on calligraphy, a source of inspiration that a medieval monk might particularly appreciate.[12]

Medieval monks had a common interest in theology, but they understood that their communities were vastly enriched by the study of other subjects in addition to scripture. Although they would not have approved of all the texts available to modern readers, they would have envied the wide range of reading material available at our fingertips, especially considering every word of their reading material was copied out by hand. With all this knowledge and entertainment available to us, and the many benefits that reading bestows, including calmness, empathy, inspiration, and pleasure, following Saint Benedict's advice and cultivating a daily reading habit is one of the simplest and most fun ways to improve our lives.

Make Peace with Your Past

> Of every age of thy life, of childhood, of youth;
> bring them all into remembrance.
> —The Ancren Riwle

Modern psychologists tell us that perhaps the most effective way to deal with difficult memories, emotions, or trauma, is not to dismiss them but to face them head-on. Suppressing negative emotions is a direct route to mental ill health and distress.[13] Medieval monks might

Baptism was one of the most important sacraments of the church, as it confirmed the person as a Christian and washed away original sin. Once sins began piling up again, however, it was important to confess them to keep the soul clean.
The Taymouth Hours, fol. 134r, 14th century (detail)
British Library, London; Yates Thompson 13

not have thought of this the same way, in that they *were* meant to dismiss negative emotions and try not to feel them during their day-to-day functioning; however, this was more to keep them from disrupting their (and others') work and concentration. They were not naïve enough to believe that negative emotions would just disappear like smoke. Instead, monks and nuns were to bring their troubles to God in quiet moments and ask for his help.

What is perhaps a key difference between modern therapy and medieval prayer is that modern people frequently are encouraged to consider troubling situations in their pasts in order to discover those parts of the situ-

Confession was central to medieval Christianity, as no one could enter heaven with sins on their conscience. Fortunately, through confession, contrition, and penance, medieval monks could wipe out past sins.

Duke Albrecht's *Table of Christian Faith* (winter part),
fol. 112v, 1400–1404 (detail)
Walters Art Museum, Baltimore; W.171

*All sins were categorized under one of the seven
deadly sins, pictured here.*
Testament, fol. 165r, c. 1380 (detail)
British Library, London; Yates Thompson 21

ation they are responsible for and to let go of those they definitely are not responsible for. On balance, a person working through a mental health issue is likely to be reminded that humans are fallible and that they shouldn't judge themselves too harshly for their mistakes.

As with so many things, the medieval take on this situation differed depending on who you asked. The medieval church believed that humans are fallible, yes, but that didn't necessarily mean that a person could be let off the hook too easily. While medieval Christians were meant to forgive each other for their sins and accept human failings, there was an emphasis on taking accountability for your own mistakes, lest you were sent to purgatory or hell for not having properly made amends. *The Ancren Riwle* puts this very bluntly: "No good that is in us is of ourselves: our good is God's; but our sin is of ourselves, and is our own."[14]

Interestingly, a common thread between both modern therapy and medieval spiritual belief is the encouragement to name the issue. People today are encouraged to name what they're feeling in order to confront it and start to work through their emotions, and studies show that they often find relief in the process of naming alone.[15] Medieval monks were encouraged in a similar way to categorize their distress into the sins they had committed. Negative emotions like wrath or envy were easy to categorize and allowed the monk at prayer or in confession to name the source of his distress—for example, realizing that the reason he hid Brother Anselm's comb was that he was envious of Anselm's looks. Naming the sin allowed proper penance to be doled out in confession, which allowed the monk to erase the sin from his divine record and release it from his conscience.

Instead of having to carry the weight of a past transgression, monks or nuns could atone for their mistakes through prayer, penance, or good works and be absolved. In a similar way, when we are confronted with those memories that disturb or distress us, we can look for the ways in which we were responsible—or not responsible—for them, name what we're feeling, and, whether with the guidance of a counselor or therapist or on our own, learn to let go.

No matter what sins a brother had committed, if he was truly contrite, he would be forgiven.
The Smithfield Decretals,
fol. 224v, late 13th–early 14th century (detail)
British Library, London; Royal 10 E IV

Be Mindful of Your Body

> The pious recluse, though she fly ever so high,
> must at times alight down to the earth in respect
> of her body—and eat, drink, sleep, work, speak,
> and hear, when it is necessary, of earthly things.
>   —The Ancren Riwle

As we've seen in our examination of the monastic garden, monks and theologians were curious about the workings of the universe, eager to understand God's plan and his masterpieces. As members of the one species believed to be made in God's own image, people interested in God quite naturally were interested in their own physiology.

Religious doctrine forbade Christians to perform autopsies, so their understanding of the inner workings of the body were dependent upon their knowledge of animal bodies, injuries, and the writings of past scholars—especially Islamic doctors, whose knowledge of medicine was far more advanced than the West's during much of the Middle Ages. Nevertheless, while the medical theories they had inherited from ancient sources like Hippocrates and Galen may make medieval people seem embarrassingly ignorant about human anatomy (oddly, the ancients never seem to shoulder the blame for these theories), medieval monks made some extremely astute observations about how bodies worked, noticing everything from how the heart pumped blood to how head injuries could cause personality changes, to how disease could sometimes be diagnosed through looking at urine samples.

Despite the monastic admiration for the workings of anatomy, human bodies were always being denigrated by monks as sinful and often punished for wanting things beyond what a monk *wanted* them to want, like extra food, extra sleep, and sex. The ways in which monks would chastise their bodies for these desires could be cruel and included anything from fasting to wearing hair shirts to flagellation. At the same time, a certain respect for the body, like every other aspect of medieval life, was firmly rooted in theology. As we've seen, contemplating the mortal body and suffering of Jesus was a fruitful and encouraged practice. Given that the body is something that is always with us and that we understand implicitly, it was also a good vehicle for explaining theology, such as in Colossians 1:18, when Christ is explained to be "the head of the body, the church."

Monks were concerned with their bodies being as perfect as possible in order to reflect God's perfection, so they preferred to receive novices who did not have physical disabilities—something that doesn't vibe well with their teachings of loving their neighbors, but that was consistent with other theological ideas around clergy and physical "perfection."[16] The paradox, of course, was that a clergyman was to be physically beautiful but not to be aware of it, as that would be vanity. (Unfortunately, in the modern world, we still seem to require that—of beautiful women, especially.)

What separates us from these monks—hopefully beyond such discrimination—is the fact that ideas of physical perfection were not tied to extreme thinness or bulging muscles. A godlike figure in the medieval imagination was not the same as what we may imagine a godlike figure to be now, perhaps as exemplified in the form of the current cinematic version of Thor. Someone with extreme muscle tone was someone who spent a lot of time doing manual labor, and while Jesus was believed to have been raised by a carpenter, he was not known for Herculean feats of strength.

Some religious ascetics, especially women, seemed to embrace the waiflike thinness that came from excessive fasting, an obsession that has been likened to "spiritual anorexia."[17] The reason for the joy in this emaciation, however, was not about wanting to look like an ideal woman (the ideal feminine form in the Middle Ages was not emaciated but somewhat "pear-shaped," in the words of modern women's magazines) but more about successfully avoiding temptation and denying pleasure in food. Advice for women, such as that in *The Ancren Riwle*, cautioned them *not* to fast too much, as it would make them unable to properly serve God, sick and weak as they would become. Moderation was much to be preferred.

The medieval monastic lifestyle, while centered around contemplation, was a more active one than we might imagine. Given that there were no machines to make everyday tasks like cooking, washing dishes, doing laundry, and keeping warm effortless, monks had a fair amount of physical labor to perform. Cistercians, in particular, determined not to be overly dependent on lay brothers to do their work for them, were also engaged in activities like agricultural work, which would keep them fit. Brothers would have had lean muscle from chopping and stacking firewood or carrying it to the dormitory; hauling buckets of water for washing hands, bodies, dishes, and clothing; or serving trays of food and drinks in the refectory.

Monks weren't worried about achieving a specific body shape: they were concerned only with having enough strength to do the things they needed to do, and this is a mindset many of us can and should take to heart. A certain amount of denial of the body's wants is a good thing, like turning down a fourth piece of cake when we're already full. It's worth considering which foods we choose to eat and then to consume them mindfully and with gratitude, but it's both unnecessary and unwise to starve ourselves or overexercise to the point of becoming sick and incapable of doing what we wish to do with our lives. Instead of obsessing over a body type that, even in our own media, is meant to be an illustration of something as unattainable as godhood, we should consider what we want the strength of our bodies to be *for*. Like monks, we can integrate activities into our daily routines that keep us strong enough to fight off disease and to do things we enjoy, like running, biking, or swimming, improving both our health and our quality of life.

Consider Staying Anonymous

> *A good action dragged before the world is not*
> *only lost through that vanity, but appeareth*
> *even loathsome in the sight of God.*
> —The Ancren Riwle

Perhaps one of the most frustrating things about being a medieval historian is trying to piece together the movements and actions of people like medieval monks through authorship. This is because the vast majority of medieval texts—especially those written in the early Middle Ages—are unattributed. Rare is the occasion on which we can point to the name of an author or copyist, leaving us reliant on clues in distinctive phrasing, spelling, or handwriting.

To the medieval mind, remaining anonymous was not done to irritate future readers and nosy historians. Rather, it was an intentional erasing of the person so that the message could come through all the clearer. There is a reason monks were instructed to dress the same way, chant the same things, eat the same food, and wear the same hairstyle beyond the practical: it was a way to embrace humility by offering up the ego. In fact, the historian's quest to dig out the individual behind the writing would probably be just as exasperating to the monks and nuns themselves, as trying to unmask them is missing the point. (Then again, our purposes are entirely different.)

In *The Dialogue on Miracles*, a monk named Caesarius of Heisterbach recorded hundreds of stories that illustrated the good—and sometimes bad—deeds of both people from history and people known to Caesarius and his contemporaries, in order to make monastic concepts like contrition and confession clearer to novices. Caesarius purposefully obscures his name in his prologue, saying, "When the name of the author is withheld, the tongue of the detractor finds nothing to feed upon";[18] that is, none of the value of the content is lost simply because someone doesn't like the author. Unable to help himself, perhaps tempted by pride or in the interest of building credibility, Caesarius *does* give a hint, beginning each section with words made up of the letters that spell out his name. Otherwise, we likely would never know it.

What's interesting about *The Dialogue on Miracles* is that even though many of the monks featured in the stories were known to either Caesarius or people he knew, most of the names in the book are obscured, replaced with only "a monk" or "a certain clerk." Sometimes this is because Caesarius says he does not know it; sometimes it's because it was against the rules to out someone else in your own confession;[19] and other times it is out of sensitivity, such as when he says, "I will not name either the knight or the monastery, lest perchance any of those I shall speak of may still be alive, and suffer shame."[20] As with the declaration in his prologue, Caesarius believes that it's unnecessary to know a person's name all the time, and it can sometimes be detrimental. The moral of the story is much more important than the author or even the actor.

This humility is seen in other places, such as those in

the work of the anchorite Julian of Norwich, who we encountered earlier. Julian has been named after the church where her anchor-hold was located—Saint Julian's—because her real name is not actually known. Even contemporary accounts of conversations with Julian, such as the one in the autobiography of a pilgrim named Margery Kempe, or in wills in which posthumous donations were made to support Julian, her name is not used, which suggests that most people did not know it even then. Julian does not feel it necessary to explain who she is in her own works, and perhaps she felt it would be detrimental to the work as well. Since she became an anchorite later in life, by her own account, Julian had decades of life from which people who wanted to discredit her could dig up skeletons. Better, then, to remain anonymous in order to keep the focus on her message of love and hope.[21] People have since quoted Julian countless times without knowing her identity, which perhaps goes to show that maybe it is irrelevant after all.

In the modern world, anonymity is wielded as a weapon, a tool, and a gift. Anonymous social media accounts provide a shield for toxic vitriol that would have horrified devout medieval monks (although this is not to say that there weren't toxic monks too). At the same time, anonymity still allows us to share things in which the message is more important than the messenger; anonymity, for example, allows victims of sexual assault or oppression to speak truth without losing their livelihoods or their lives.

These days, we are encouraged to live our individualism loudly and proudly, and that is a wonderful freedom that many people in the medieval world never got to experience. But there are moments when it's important to quieten our own voices in order to lift up those of others—to retweet rather than quote tweet, to amplify, not take the spotlight. For medieval monks, these moments came often and in the service of holy texts, whose messages were fundamentally about the elevation of collective spiritual well-being over the individual. For modern people, it's worth taking a moment to think before we bring attention to ourselves, about whether the messages we're trying to convey are better served without our egos muddying the waters.

Practice Gratitude

> What is sweeter to us, dearest brothers, than this voice of the Lord inviting us? Look: the Lord in his love shows us the way of life.
> —Benedict of Nursia, *The Rule of Saint Benedict*

At the center of Christianity is the promise that people who believe in Jesus and who are contrite in their hearts will be given an eternity of peace, comfort, and joy. That the promise is available to any and all who meet these conditions is a source of earthly peace, comfort, and joy for the faithful, and the reason for a tremendous amount of spiritual gratitude. Although thankfulness for the eternal life that awaited them made up the core of medieval monks' practice of gratitude, monks were also in the habit of turning their thoughts to gratitude many times a day for both the big things and the small things.

The medieval period was a difficult time to be alive by all accounts. In an era before temperature-controlled homes, supermarkets, and antibiotics, people were much more at the mercy of environmental factors—a season that was simply too rainy, for example, could lead to cold, famine, and death. They understood, perhaps better than we do today, that each breath, each meal, each moment with a friend is a blessing for which to be grateful.

The crucifixes to be found all over monasteries allowed for regular reflection on holy themes.
Omne Bonum (Absolucio-Circumcisio), fol. 409v, c. 1360–75 (detail)
British Library, London; Royal 6 E VI

Monastic gratitude was simple in many ways. Without God, nothing would exist at all. Without Jesus, everyone would be damned to hell for eternity. With that perspective, it's hard not to be grateful. Human nature being what it is, however, even monks needed reminders.

One recent trend to remind modern people to be grateful for all the good in our own lives is to carry a rock in a pocket as a literal touchstone of gratitude. Every time we reach in to get keys, or coins, or just tuck our hands in, the rock is there to give us a nudge to take a moment and be grateful. In a similar way, medieval monks reminded themselves of the sacrifice of Jesus, for which they were always to be thankful, by using the sign of the cross. There were crucifixes to be found everywhere, from the church to the dormitory, and as we learned from the master of Barnwell Priory's instructions for the novice, every time they sat, the brothers folded their robes into the form of the cross. Barnwell's novice was taught even more ways to be reminded of the Crucifixion throughout the day, such as,

> how when he goes to bed he ought to sign himself and his bed thrice with the sign of the cross, and again when he gets up, how he should fortify himself with the same sign…how he should never take food unless it have been first blessed by himself or by another and how, after food, he should give thanks to God.[22]

All these small moments and gestures were meant to refocus a brother's mind on the reason he had these blessings in the first place, so that he might be appropriately grateful, no matter how he actually felt about the early hour or day thirty-six of having Lenten eels on his plate.

Too much repetition can make symbolic gestures lose their meaning, of course, just like we might soon learn to ignore the rock in our pocket from overexposure to it. But we can also just as easily snap back into remembering why we have that habit in the first place, especially if, like medieval monks, we see it being done by other people.

Modern studies have shown that practicing gratitude in the morning or before bedtime has positive effects on people's moods and on their success.[23] Taking a few moments to be thankful before we start our days, or as we end them, increases happiness overall. Although nothing more than a pause for reflection is needed, experts suggest that writing down three to five things for which we're grateful is a good idea and gives us a record of pleasant things to look back on if we find ourselves struggling on a different day. Fortunately for us, we don't need to find ourselves expensive parchment to do it: we can use scrap paper or sticky notes, buy ourselves one of the many beautiful gratitude journals for sale, or download an app that gives us helpful notifications. However we integrate gratitude into our lives, following the monastic example of making it a daily habit will bring us more happiness—and more success—in the long run.

Keep the Faith

> Let no one think that he can ascend to the
> stars with luxurious ease.
> —*The Ancren Riwle*

Although the monastic life was meant to make it easier for a person to keep their faith at all times, surrounded by other faithful brothers and sisters with the same concentrated focus, in reality, monks and nuns were plagued by doubt and temptation.

It's not surprising, given the difficulty intentionally placed on the faithful, that doubts haunted them during cold nights, seemingly endless fasts, and mind-numbing routine. Not the mindless automatons they're so often portrayed to be in modern media, these were real humans who occasionally asked themselves what all their deprivation was for. In a culture in which doubt and despair themselves were sinful, the combined weight of daily hardship and guilt over their lack of faith sometimes drove members of monastic communities to quit or even commit suicide.

The particular despair that came of monastic boredom and a feeling of pointlessness was called "accidie" (or "acedia"). Caesarius describes this emotion for a novice, saying,

Accidie is a depression born from a troubled mind; or a sense of weariness and excessive bitterness of heart, by which spiritual happiness is cast out, and the judgement is overthrown by a headlong fall into dispair [sic]. It is called accidie, as if it were an acid, which makes all spiritual exercises bitter and insipid to us.... The progeny of accidie or depression are: malice, rancour, cowardice, despair, reluctance to obey, and the straying of the thoughts into forbidden places. Accidie is a common temptation and throws many into despair.[24]

He then goes on to tell stories of monks who, suffering from accidie, struggle to get out of bed or to perform their duties.

Although spiritual leaders condemned accidie, they understood it and did their best to mitigate the problem. Brothers at Barnwell Priory who were overwhelmed or depressed by the current moment were told to take a short break to clear their minds and restore their mental health with walks and visits with brothers they were close to:

Brethren sometimes fall into a state of weak health from the irksomeness of life in the Cloister, or from long continuance of silence; sometimes from fatigue in the [choir] or extension of fasting; sometimes from sleeplessness or overwork.... Those afflicted with these and similar infirmities cannot read or sing, or perform properly any of the other duties pertaining to the Observances directed by the Rule. On account of such an attack, however, they ought not to go into the [infirmary], or to stay there, because they do not require medicine, but only repose and comfort. [With permission] they may walk in the vineyard, the garden, and along the riverside [or] they

may go beyond the precincts into the fields, mead-
ows, woods, or any other place…and even, for their
diversion, take their meals with those who have been
bled; they may absent themselves, for a short time,
from the [choir], from study, and from the Cloister,
and so, by repose, diet, and recreation, regain before
long their former state of health.[25]

It's clear that, while the church did take a hard line on
despair, believing as it did that a person in despair no longer had faith in God's plan or his wisdom, monks and
spiritual advisers felt compassion for those who were
struggling.

In addition to being given rest and a break from their
duties, monks were reminded that suffering was to be
expected as part of their vocation. Being sorely tested
is a good thing, they were assured, and it happens to everyone. "Here is another encouragement which ought
greatly to comfort you when ye are tempted," writes the
author of The Ancren Riwle:

The tower is not attacked, nor the castle, nor the city,
after they are taken; even so the warrior of hell at-
tacks, with temptation, none whom he hath in his
hand; but he attacketh those whom he hath not.[26]

Being tempted or feeling accidie are not reasons for a
brother to give up, because they mean that he is still in the
fight. Temptation itself is not a failure; it is a challenge to
overcome.

What these writers are suggesting is not a change in circumstances but a shift in perspective: instead of focusing
on the hardship, focus on the opportunity. Instead of feeling self-pity, see if you can find what can be learned from
the situation.

Just as we must be mindful of the type of talk we listen to and engage in, we must also be aware of the ways we frame our own difficulties. Modern psychology has shown that shifting perspective can allow a person to manage hardship better, not only in the moment but in future struggles as well. Few things are more harmful to mental health than repetitively dwelling on negative thoughts.[27] Although it can be very difficult to snap out of rumination on our own, people in medieval monasteries were on the lookout for those sinking into accidie and were practiced in intervening to help realign a struggling brother's worldview to one in which he could find peace with his situation. We can do the same for ourselves and for our friends, training ourselves to notice when we ruminate and gently realigning our thoughts to stop the spiral.

Whatever our spiritual beliefs, the kernel of wisdom from *The Ancren Riwle* is a worthwhile one to hold onto in times of hardship. Everyone will struggle in life; there is not one exception to this rule. But the tower does not remain under siege if the battle is already won. We will not always feel sad or afflicted, much as it may seem that way sometimes. As long as there is life, there is hope that things will get better, and when we focus on that hope, we are already on the path out of the darkness.

IV
LOOK
OUTWARD

So great efficacy hath love and good will, that it maketh the good which it doth to another our own, as well as his.

—*The Ancren Riwle*

 critical component of medieval Christianity was service. In the modern world, we're aware of the importance of community and of working toward a common purpose, perhaps even more so since we've had to stay apart during the COVID-19 pandemic. A medieval monk might seem like the last person to have any involvement or investment in the world outside the cloister walls; however, there were countless ways in which monks and nuns worked to improve the lives of the people in their communities—and even those of people today.

Share Your Knowledge

> *While the mind is still easy to mold and as*
> *pliable as wax, taking the form of what is*
> *impressed upon it, it should be exercised from*
> *the very beginning in every good discipline.*
> —Saint Basil, *The Long Rules*

Since medieval Christians believed that everyone on earth is a sinner from the moment they're born and that sin without repentance leads to eternal damnation, it's not surprising that members of the clergy were deeply concerned with spreading the word of God to everyone they could in order to save as many souls as possible. One of the most effective ways of doing this was to provide education.

Although mothers were children's first teachers, just as they so often are today, formal education was provided in

The three boys being rescued here by Saint Nicholas appear to be schoolboys, as their tonsures bear out.
Prayer book, fol. 164v, c. 1430–40 (detail)
Walters Art Museum, Baltimore; W.164

cathedrals and monasteries during much of the Middle Ages. Like the boys who were sent to be fostered in other homes to begin their knightly training, boys who were sent to monastic schools began their learning around the age of seven.[1] Girls were taught either by their mothers or tutors at home, or much more rarely, by nuns at a convent. For girls, a formal education was usually a direct route to becoming a nun, while boys had many career opportunities available to them.

Children in school were first taught Latin, so that they could learn their prayers and the psalms, as well as the other songs they were meant to perform as part of church services. Latin had long replaced Greek (at least in the West) as the language of academia and of holy texts. It was the language in which the learned spoke and wrote, from members of the clergy to members of the court, many of whom were both at the same time. For a monk to absorb the mysteries of the Mass, and the teachings of the church fathers, it was essential for him to at least learn to read Latin and understand it as a spoken language. Writing was considered a separate skill, and not all monks learned it.

In addition to Latin, monks learned math, music, and some science, as well as how to argue logically and con-

A monastic education prepared boys not only for a life in the cloister but also for higher education and a career as a doctor or a lawyer (pictured on the left).

Omne Bonum (Absolucio-Circumcisio), fol. 50v, c. 1360–75 (detail)
British Library, London; Royal 6 E VI

One of the skills taught in the medieval curriculum was rhetoric, the ability to make a clear and convincing argument, an important skill for all clergy to learn.
Scholastic miscellany, fol. 218v,
1309–16 (detail)
British Library, London; Burney 275

vincingly. Although the Middle Ages is widely reputed to have been a time when people blindly followed religious dogma, in reality, there were constant debates about the nature of faith, heaven and hell, the divinity and humanity of Jesus, and how best to serve God. Ordinary people expected the clergy to have the answers to their questions, so it was vital that monks not only learned their theology but also learned how to explain it in a way that did not lead to misunderstanding or more doubt.

Young students (clerks) sometimes lived within the precinct in order to study under the care of the almoner, who was in charge of the abbey's charitable works. The *Observances* of Barnwell Priory give us a glimpse into what schooling was like there:

> Those clerks who live on charity, and are housed in the Almonry, should often be set to argue against each other by the Almoner, or some person connected with his office, and be kept under the rod, that they may learn better; and on feast days, when they do not go to school, he should strictly command them to read and sing in church, to commit to memory the Mattins of Blessed Mary, to learn to write on parchment, and to repeat by heart their

Boys who were educated in the monastery were expected to behave themselves "instead of running about in the streets, or fighting," as the Observances of Barnwell Priory tells us.

Scholastic miscellany, fol. 256v, 1309–16 (detail)
British Library, London; Burney 275

letters, and their lines to explain the different meanings of words, instead of running about in the streets, or fighting, or disputing. Otherwise, the Almoner ought to turn them out as unfit persons, and substitute well-conducted scholars in their room.[2]

These rambunctious clerks were not integrated into the monastic community for the most part, although they did participate in church services as altar boys.[3] As we saw earlier, boys were considered to be too disruptive and distracting, and besides, many of them would not take vows in the end, leaving the monastery in their late teens to go to university to become priests, teachers, doctors, or lawyers.

It's clear from their being housed at the monastery, despite their potential for trouble, how important it was to the monastic community to educate young men. By giving them a foundation in theology, the monks were teaching them to live a moral life; by giving them small roles in church services, the monks were showing them responsibility; and by giving them the skills to read and write, the monks were providing them the tools with which to build successful careers. Students could grow up to become archbishops, advisers to kings, or even saints, like Thomas Becket, who, with a monastic education, managed to become all three.

Not all of us are made to be teachers in a formal sense, but we all have gifts and knowledge to share with others. If, like our monastic brethren, we consider education to be both our privilege and our responsibility, we can take the opportunity to share our talents, shaping each other's minds and skill sets like wax, as Saint Basil suggests, and leaving a lasting impression.

Write Your Memoirs

> I have been concerned here to record what I know from personal experience of the events that took place in St. Edmund's church in my time, describing the bad deeds as well as the good, to provide both warning and example.
> —Jocelin of Brakelond,
> Chronicle of the Abbey of Bury St Edmunds

During the first few months of the COVID-19 pandemic, when events were happening quickly and people were struggling to process their emotions and understand the rules, historians took to social media to encourage people to write down their experiences as they happened. Firsthand accounts are some of the most valuable pieces of evidence we have to reconstruct historical events and to understand them. In the Middle Ages, a time when people were dealing with their own climate shifts, political unrest, and pandemics, it was monks who did the lion's share of chronicling events for posterity.

While monks were very much invested in copying existing works to share with others in their order and in the wider world (as we'll see shortly), they were also in-

terested in making sure their own collective stories were
recorded. In part, this was history for history's sake—that
is, making sure that future generations had a picture of
events as they happened—but they wanted an accounting
of history for all sorts of other reasons too: to commemo-
rate events, to record miracles performed by local saints
or witnessed by contemporaries, and to settle disputes regarding property, to name a few. In fact, monasteries were
so concerned with establishing paper trails for their own

*Some of the medieval manuscripts that still exist today are
copies of chronicles or monastic histories, like this copy of
the* Lives of Saints Edmund and Fremund *presented to
Henry VI.*

Lives of Saints Edmund and Fremund, fol. 6r, c. 1434–39 (detail)
British Library, London; Harley 2278

histories that they occasionally forged documents to support them.[4]

The contents of monastic chronicles run the gamut from the most mundane information about internal elections to weather reports, to snippy commentaries on royals like King John, to chilling records of the monks who died, one by one, of the Black Death. Sometimes there are demonic sightings, sometimes there are ghost stories, and sometimes there are gossipy swipes at the abbot. Occasionally, we get a passage that gives us a human face to put to a name, as in this description of the twelfth-century abbot of Bury Saint Edmunds, who we met in chapter two:

> Abbot Samson was of medium height and almost completely bald. His face was neither round nor long, and he had a prominent nose and thick lips. His eyes were crystal clear, with a penetrating gaze, and he had extremely sharp hearing. His eyebrows were bushy and were frequently trimmed. As soon as he caught a slight cold he became hoarse. On the day of his election [to the abbacy, February 28, 1182] he was 47 years of age, and had been a monk for seventeen years. There were then only a few grey hairs in his red beard and very few indeed in his hair, which was black and wavy, but within fourteen years of his election he had turned as white as snow. He was a very serious-minded man and was never idle. His health was excellent, and he liked to travel on horseback or on foot, until he was prevented by old age.[5]

Portraits like this remind us of the humanity within the monastery and of the value of understanding a person's physical presence and how he presents himself to others. Although facial recognition may soon make the practice obsolete, reflecting on a written portrait such as this one brings home the importance of recording the names of the loved ones in our own photographs before they are lost to history.

Monastic chronicles are an absolute treasure trove of information for historians, as they tell us not only about the happenings both inside and outside the monastery but also the values of the monks: their likes and dislikes, what they were willing to tolerate and not tolerate, and what their attitudes were toward society, technology, and life in general.

Jocelin of Brakelond's chronicle of Bury Saint Edmunds provides another good example of this when he recounts the time a candle guttered out and set the shrine of Saint Edmund on fire shortly before matins one night in 1198. His account is full of interesting detail:

> Our young monks ran for water, some to the rainwater tank, some to the clock, and some, with great difficulty, when they had snatched up the reliquaries, put out the flames with their hoods. When cold water was thrown on the front of the shrine, the precious stones fell down and were almost pulverized.

This tiny snippet gives us a glimpse into the monks' life, letting us know they collected water in rain barrels and they used a water clock. Jocelin also goes on to describe how the monks secretly hired a goldsmith to repair the shrine "to avoid public disgrace," and how the abbot later blamed the incident on divine punishment for the monks' "complaints about the food and drink." Jocelin, on paper at least, disagreed with this unfair interpretation. He believed that the fire had occurred so that the saint's body would be placed "more safely and more spectacularly in a higher position."[6]

As Jocelin's explanation demonstrates, monks were

*According to Jocelin of Brakelond, the shrine of Saint
Edmund (pictured) was secretly repaired after it was
damaged by fire.*
Lives of Saints Edmund and Fremund, fol. 9r, c. 1434–39 (detail)
British Library, London; Harley 2278

always invested in trying to understand the big picture.
Nearly every philosophical structure they built for understanding the world could be used allegorically, as a way of
exploring the story of Jesus's life and as a way of understanding the astounding synchronicity of the universe—
beautiful patterns that repeated everywhere and seemed
to confirm the existence of God. Chronicling allowed
monks, as well as contemporary and future readers, to
put events into context. As Caesarius wished to show
in his *Dialogue on Miracles*, the morals of our stories are
made clear with hindsight, and in them the workings of
God are revealed.

For the modern person, chronicling the events of just
the past few years and trying to make sense of them might
seem like a Herculean task, but with that massive effort
being undertaken by professional historians and journal-
ists, we can focus on our own lives in a journaling habit.
Even a line a day can trigger our memories and give us

the benefit of hindsight to see how far we've come, what we've lived through, and how it affected us. Although we can review our challenges and funny moments in part by reading back over the posts we've made on social media as we lived through them, as anyone who's tried to access an old file knows, digital writing can be far more ephemeral than a paper record. In this, perhaps, we should definitely take a page, as it were, from our medieval monastic brothers and write our thoughts and observations by hand to better preserve them for the future.

Beyond recording our thoughts for posterity, however, studies have shown that journaling helps us by giving us the opportunity to frame our own narratives in a way that allows us to understand and accept the events we live through, much as we saw how reframing allowed monks to push through challenging times. For the faithful or philosophical, journaling may indeed be an avenue by which we can come to understand the workings of the universe or the divine in our own lives. The lessons we learn from the events we record can be shared to help both us and our future readers find meaning and motivation.

Embrace Innovation

> Ye ought not, like unwise people, to promise to
> keep any of the external rules.... Ye may even
> change them, whenever ye will, for better ones.
> —The Ancren Riwle

One of the most consistent and misguided beliefs about the medieval world is that the church was opposed to science and technology. Like the myth that medieval people believed Earth was flat, this is one that can be easy to disprove, although making the effort can be rewarding because of just how fascinating it is to explore the

Far from being reviled or feared, science was devotional: it was monks' way of understanding how God had designed the universe. Here, God uses a compass as he creates a spherical Earth.

Image du Monde, fol. 9v, 1489 (detail)
Walters Art Museum, Baltimore; W.199

Medieval people's understanding of science was remarkably sophisticated in many ways, as this diagram explaining a solar eclipse reveals.

Image du Monde, fol. 98v, 1489 (detail)
Walters Art Museum, Baltimore; W.199

*Perhaps above all other sciences, monks embraced astronomy, which
gave them the knowledge they needed to tell time, navigate, and
predict celestial events. This is likely a picture of Lady Astronomy
revealing her secrets.*

Scholastic miscellany, fol. 390v, 1309–16 (detail)
British Library, London; Burney 275

ways in which technology flourished during this period,
thanks in large part to the curiosity of monks.

Perhaps the most vivid example of monasteries driving
innovation is their use of clocks. Monks, as well as other
members of the clergy and the especially devout, were
meant to sing and chant specific psalms and prayers at certain hours of the day—the canonical hours—as we've seen.
Although they're called "hours," they were not set out in
the sixty-minute intervals we use today but at points that

*While medieval monks got many things right, they did believe in
an Earth-centered universe (in part for spiritual reasons). This
diagram shows the planets in their celestial spheres.*
Image du Monde, fol. 91v, 1489 (detail)
Walters Art Museum, Baltimore; W.199

would ebb and flow with the length of the daylight hours
throughout the year. For the sacrist, in charge of calling
the monks to prayer, it was critical to know when to ring
the bells for services despite their changing with the sea-
sons, so the church was invested in anything that would
provide reliable timekeeping.

Medieval monks invented and used all sorts of inge-
nious methods to keep track of time, including candles
marked with hourly increments that could be measured

as they burned down; sundials; hourglasses; water clocks, whose rate of drainage tracked the time and eventually sounded an alarm; astrolabes, which could also calculate location, among other things; and mechanical clocks, driven by weights (as in Salisbury Cathedral) or by winding. Mechanical clocks found their homes in churches and monasteries well before it became the fashion to install them in town squares.[7] Believe it or not, it was the church's acceptance of, and active push for, better timekeeping that led directly to our time-obsessed modern culture.[8]

It wasn't just clocks that monks embraced, however. Improved waterwheels, better rabbit hutches, and new methods for organizing content in books—including tables of contents and alphabetization—all were ways in which monks followed their curiosity about the world in order to create and implement new solutions to old problems. In some medieval manuscripts, the gospel writers themselves are poster children for medieval technological innovation, such as the venerable Saint Mark, who appears at his desk modeling a newfangled twelfth-century innovation: eyeglasses.

Saint Mark models the church's acceptance of technology by sporting a medieval invention: eyeglasses.
The Tilliot Hours, fol. 12r, c. 1500 (detail)
British Library, London; Yates Thompson 5

The fact that monks embraced innovation should come as no surprise to us, really. Like us, monks were invested in anything that would make life simpler and easier, streamlining daily tasks so that they could focus on the devotional practices to which they had dedicated their lives.

Modern technology is meant to serve the same purpose: saving us time and effort in order to help our lives run smoothly and simply enough that we can focus on the things that are important to us. It's often worthwhile to take a little time to learn a new way of doing things or to figure out a new app that will help make our lives easier. Sometimes, experimenting in efficiency backfires, as we fill the time we've saved with other activities that may not be meaningful to us, in which case, perhaps, we have to return to our monkish lessons on minimalism (chapter two). But it's human nature to explore ways to make our lives better, improving other people's lives with the spillover. When we share our "life hacks" with the rest of the world, we're following in the footsteps of our monastic brethren by embracing innovation for the sake of a better world for ourselves and for others.

Help Those in Need

Care should be taken for the sick before all and above all.
—Benedict of Nursia, *The Rule of Saint Benedict*

The modern world makes a big deal of separating faith and science, while in the medieval world the two were in many ways inseparable, as we've seen. With this in mind, perhaps it's not surprising by this point in our journey to discover that the first medieval hospitals were opened and run by monks and nuns. This makes sense in part because monasteries had infrastructure and funding that were transferable—an easier prospect than trying

The almoner was in charge of distributing monastic money to the poor and needy. This lockable alms box with a coin slot in the top prevented people from helping themselves to Christian charity.
Alms box, 15th century
The Met Cloisters, New York

to start a project like a hospital from scratch—but it also makes sense because of the spiritual obligation monks had to charity.

It may surprise modern people to know, however, that one of the most significant hospitals in the medieval world—the Hospital of Saint John of Jerusalem in Jerusalem—opened its doors to both Christians and non-Christians alike. Anyone could be treated there for illness or injury; however, Jewish and Muslim patients would have to submit to their caregivers dispensing Christian theology as well as medicine. In the minds of these monastic nurses, caring for the soul of the patients was actually more important than caring for their bodies, as bodies are transient, but the afterlife is forever.

Monks—or, more frequently, nuns—were the ones who staffed medieval hospitals, where they literally ministered to the sick, giving them spiritual comfort as well as medical aid. There was much to be done in or-

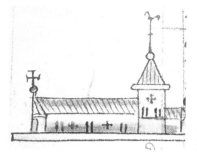

As this marginal picture of a hospital shows, the care patients received there was as focused on spiritual health as physical health.

Historia Anglorum, fol. 121v, 1250–59 (detail)
British Library, London; Royal 14 C VII

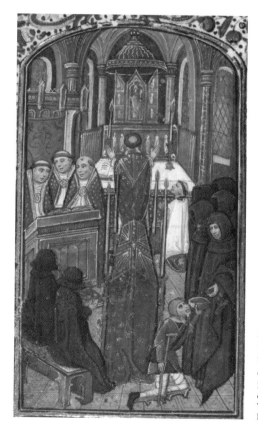

Monastic charity extended to people who might have trouble making ends meet due to poverty or disability.

Book of hours, fol. 120v, c. 1460–70 (detail)
Walters Art Museum, Baltimore; W.181

Ministering spiritually to the sick could be beneficial to the monastery too, as in this picture, where an ailing clerk considers joining the abbey.
Decretum, fol. 207v, late 13th–early 14th century (detail)
British Library, London; Royal 11 D IX

der to run a medieval hospital, such as supplying food, beds, bedding, and medicine, as well as hiring staff, from university-trained medical doctors to laundresses. Although medieval hospitals are not places in which most modern people would want to find themselves, given that the lack of antiseptic, anesthesia, and antibiotics meant that conditions were definitely not as sanitary, comfortable, or sterile as those in today's hospitals, patients at the Hôtel Dieu in Paris, for example, could count on a bed with sheets that were regularly washed,[9] warm meals, and spiritual care. The word "hospital" comes from the same root as "hospitality," and the impulse to provide for people in distress the way religious orders thoughtfully hosted guests in the monastery was at the core of the care given by monks and nuns in the hospital too. Medieval hospitals were more than just places to heal the sick: they were places that provided long-term care for people who were impoverished or elderly, or those with disabilities. They were also places where poor mothers could give birth.[10]

Most monks and nuns were not formally trained to be professional nurses or doctors, but they could learn much of what they needed to know on their feet while doing the job itself. What they had instead of formal training was a

*Monks and nuns had a duty to care for the community that
included distributing alms and food and ministering to the sick.*
The Abingdon Apocalypse, fol. 30r, late 13th century (detail)
British Library, London; Additional 42555

heartfelt desire to help those people who were in need by
bringing whatever humble gifts they had to offer, whether
it was the ability to do menial tasks, like fetching, carrying, or cleaning; the sincere empathy and compassion
it takes to hold the hands of the sick or dying and bring
them peace; or the ability to bring spiritual ease to those
who were in pain or afraid. When we're sick, it can be the
smallest things that bring us relief and comfort, and little
gestures of genuine care can be almost as helpful as a visit
from the doctor.

So often, we question our own ability to bring aid to
the sick or impoverished: we are not trained; we don't
have any special gifts; we don't have money to give. From
the monastic example, however, we can learn that it isn't
always the people who are most experienced who can

Saint Matthew writes using a slanted desk of the type found in medieval monasteries. These desks made it easier for the ink to flow well from the quill.
Book of hours, fol. 43r, c. 1500 (detail)
Walters Art Museum, Baltimore; W.427

Manuscripts for devotional purposes, study, and distribution were all copied painstakingly by hand, as Saint Luke is doing here.
Hours of Duke Adolph of Cleves, fol. 94r, c. 1480–90 (detail)
Walters Art Museum, Baltimore, W.439

bring the most comfort and healing. There is something we can all contribute to those who are in need, even if it's as simple as sincere good wishes, a listening ear, and compassion.

Create Art That Lifts the Soul

If there are artisans in the monastery, they should, if the abbot permits, ply their crafts with all humility.
—Benedict of Nursia, *The Rule of Saint Benedict*

One of the most important contributions medieval monks made to the world was their diligent and skillful creation of books. Although their role in the copying and distribution of manuscripts was eventually overtaken by professional scribes—even for their own books—many of the most beautiful and richly illuminated manuscripts that have survived the Middle Ages were the product of thousands of hours put in by hun-

Copying holy books gave illuminators and scribes the chance to pour their devotion into their art, as the exquisite colors and designs of the Lindisfarne Gospels show.
The Lindisfarne Gospels, fol. 211r, c. 700–975
British Library, London; Cotton MS Nero D IV

dreds of monks,[11] bent over their desks in the well-lit rooms of their scriptoria.

Medieval Europeans wrote on parchment, thin leather made from the skin of calves, sheep, or sometimes goats, which was painstakingly tanned, stretched, scraped, and bleached to form a velvety surface that absorbed ink ex-

The vibrant art in this stunning book of hours is meant to showcase both the devotion and the wealth of its aristocratic patron.

The Limbourg Brothers (active 1399–1416), *The Belles Heures of Jean, duc de Berry*, fol. 30r, 1405–8/9
The Met Cloisters, New York

tremely well. Ink was likewise painstakingly made from everything from charcoal to oak galls, mixed with other plant materials and minerals to make pigment. Paint involved a similar combination of colorful minerals or plants, thickened with egg whites to go on more smoothly and cover larger areas. Finally, many medieval manuscripts were embellished with gold leaf, pasted on with gesso and polished to a high shine. Like the Gothic churches mentioned earlier, these were works of art, the effort put in devoted to God.[12]

Monks copied all sorts of manuscripts, borrowed from and traded with sister houses, a variety of which we've already discussed. These copies were sometimes created for the monks themselves, to supplement an abbey's library or to supply a loaner textbook to a brother sent to study at university, for example. In other cases, the books were commissioned by wealthy nobles or royalty, or they were gifts made by the monks for individual citizens or for churches.

In addition to brilliantly illuminated copies of biblical texts like the world-famous Book of Kells and the Lindisfarne Gospels, some of the most beautiful manuscripts were commissioned books of hours, which contained the prayers that were meant to be said at the canonical hours each day. These books could be simply written in brown or black ink, or lavishly illustrated with bright colors, illustrative miniatures, and illuminated initials. They could be large copies, meant to signify both wealth and ostentatious devotion, or they could be small enough to hang from a lady's belt in a leather pouch for frequent access throughout the day.

In addition to prayers, monks frequently copied out calendars, which would allow the reader to keep track of important saints' days and feasts. The most important dates were usually written in red, which gives us both

Books of hours often contained a calendar of saints' days with important feasts marked out in red: the original red-letter days. Here, September features Saint Giles's day in red and the more important feast of Our Lady (Notre Dame) in gold, one of the many celebrations of Mary throughout the year.

Book of hours, fol. 9r, c. 1470 (detail)
Walters Art Museum, Baltimore; W.195

the word "rubric" and the phrase "red-letter day," as usually days written in red were holidays (holy days), when people would be celebrating, not working.

Since the process of copying was both arduous and

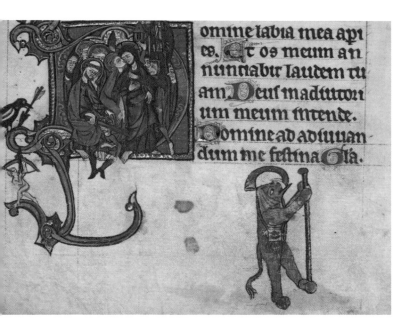

Blank space presented irresistible opportunities for colorful and irreverent marginalia, even in the most serious manuscripts. Although this page describes the betrayal of Jesus, the margin features a cheerful elephant dressed as a pilgrim in the funeral procession of Reynard the Fox.
Book of hours, fol. 73v, late 13th century (detail)
Walters Art Museum, Baltimore; W.102

time-consuming, monks didn't usually waste their time copying frivolous information; they were sharing information that they thought other people should know.

Likewise, the illustrations in medieval manuscripts weren't created solely for decoration, but for teaching and for meditation. While it's reasonable to assume that the recipients of most manuscripts were literate, not everyone who viewed them was. The illustrations that accompanied texts were therefore another way in which the stories and lessons could be shared and understood. Pictures are powerful memory aids, serving to solidify the words that a reader takes in. But medieval images were

also meant to represent holy objects themselves, sometimes containing the power of what they depicted. For example, pages on which the wounds of Jesus were vividly
painted prompted viewers to meditate on his suffering in
addition to the words on the page. Medieval readers also
frequently kissed the holy pictures in their books as part
of their devotion.[13]

Not all illustrations in medieval manuscripts were rev-
erent or holy, however. Some were playful and silly—art
for entertainment or simply for art's sake. These mostly
took the form of marginalia, colorful creatures and scenes
that surrounded the text. Even some of the most holy
words could share a page with a knightly monkey, a killer
rabbit, or an irreverent monk.

Manuscripts, then, were a way of sharing art and expression for the purpose of lifting people up, either by ele-
vating the spirit or by encouraging laughter. Medieval art,
like modern art, can be sublime or silly, the work of hours
of effort or the work of a moment's impulse. When we see
the absurdity of some marginalia, it should serve to remind us that art is human expression that is to be shared,
no matter what our skill level or what it is we like to create.

V
EVERYTHING IN MODERATION, INCLUDING MODERATION

All tasks should be done in moderation.
   —Benedict of Nursia, *The Rule of Saint Benedict*

lthough stern abbots would likely have disapproved of Oscar Wilde in general, they would have definitely (if grudgingly) recognized that he had a point in his take that everything should be in moderation, including moderation. While life in the monastery was heavy on rules, it was also understood that people aren't particularly good at being good all the time. Even *The Rule of Saint Benedict* has built-in exceptions to many of his edicts, and we know from the thunderous letters by popes and great theologians that have survived from the Middle Ages that things were often left to slide in the real day-to-day world of the monastery. So, what can we learn from this acceptance of imperfection? And how can we apply it to our lives today?

Avoid Burnout

> *Keep yourselves in such rest that long thereafter ye*
> *may labour the more vigorously in God's service.*
> —*The Ancren Riwle*

In chapter three, we saw some of the ways in which monks dealt in times when they felt down or depressed, moments that are common to us all. Living the extreme lifestyle of a medieval monk could easily lead to burnout; however, burnout was not inevitable. In the abbey, brothers were encouraged to pace themselves and scale their activities to their abilities, advice that is still worth following in our busy lives today.

One way to ensure we're not taking on more than we can handle is to ease ourselves into commitments. As we saw earlier, monastic novices were given a year to live with the brethren before they made their choice whether to stay or to go. This was because, as anyone who's suddenly jumped wholeheartedly into a new fitness regime can attest, it's very easy in the first blush of enthusiasm to

Even standing for services could be done in moderation, as these cheeky choir stalls attest. Built-in ledges allowed tired monastic bottoms to rest during long services.
Choir stalls, c. 15th century
The Met Cloisters, New York

Although monks were meant to push themselves to become learned, it was understood that grace was accessible to all, as with this monk who is blessed by Mary despite knowing only one prayer (Ave Maria).
The Taymouth Hours, fol. 161r, 14th century (detail)
British Library, London; Yates Thompson 13

bite off more than we can chew. *The Ancren Riwle* likens this to a "courtship" period, in which things are easy, acknowledging that things get considerably harder as time goes on.[1] A novice's yearlong probationary period was meant to push him past the point of any naïve initial optimism, so that he could get a sense of the difficulty he was signing up for before it was too late to go back on his word. As an additional insurance policy at Benedictine houses, *The Rule of Saint Benedict* was to be read to the novice in its entirety every few months during his novitiate, to ensure he knew exactly what was in store. Knowing what to expect made it easier for a novice to decide whether or not he could realistically commit to all a monastic life entailed once the shine had worn off.

Pushing ourselves too hard can lead to mental and physical health issues, and this was specifically warned against by monastic writers. Caesarius tells of a monk named Baldwin who ignored the warnings of the senior brothers about his overzealousness:

Not everyone could handle being a monk. Some people left the monastery, like this figure who has cast off his robes in favor of a sword. A monk could return no more than three times, according to The Rule of Saint Benedict.

Omne Bonum (Absolucio-Circumcisio), fol. 115, c. 1360–75 (detail)
British Library, London; Royal 6 E VI

For the whole year of his probation, he showed himself so scrupulous, that the abbot and the master of the novices often remonstrated with him. Further, when he became a monk, he was so full of fervour that the ordinary observances were not enough for him, and he added to them many special and private devotions. When the others ceased from labour, he still toiled, when the rest were sleeping, he still watched.[2]

While it may seem like this is the type of exemplary behavior that a monk would applaud, Baldwin's story is a cautionary one, instead, as his "indiscreet fervour" led to "violent headaches" that prompted him to attempt suicide.

Baldwin's tale vividly illustrates how working too hard can lead to illness, which actually defeats the purpose of work in the first place. Saint Benedict says repeatedly in his *Rule* that people are to be given both privileges and job assignments based on what they're capable of. Even *The Ancren Riwle*, a text dedicated to the most extreme religious life, that of the anchorite, advises it is better to rest if you're sick, "for it is great folly, for the sake of one day, to lose ten or twelve."[3] Although the self-care advised in chapter three was meant to help brothers deal with emotional low points, and definitely helped brothers who were burning out to get themselves back on track, the wisest course of action was for them to pace themselves so that they didn't burn out in the first place.

While most of us don't dedicate our lives to religion, we do live in a culture that valorizes an extreme work ethic. People who choose to work while sick, keep working far into the night, and take calls no matter where they are or what they're doing are touted as heroes to be admired. We all know people—perhaps we *are* people—who have worked themselves into ill health, and yet we still have to consciously remind ourselves that this is counterproductive, leading as it does to sick days and burnout. Overwork is so ingrained in us that it can be difficult to take a step back and realize that, in many cases, we have a choice as to how much time we dedicate to work. Of all the advice in this book, avoiding burnout by pacing ourselves might be the hardest to implement, as doing so goes against values that we see encouraged everywhere and practices that are entrenched in many a business. But if people who revered a lifestyle as extreme as medieval monks did can find a way to slow down and set achievable goals that take their

mental and physical health into account, so can we—and
so can the companies we work for.

Set Healthy Boundaries

> *You should either have no quarrels, or end them with all*
> *speed, lest anger grow into hatred.*
> —Augustine of Hippo, *The Rule of Saint Augustine*

The medieval church tends to be thought of as one
of the ultimate symbols of intolerance and sup-
pression, and sometimes its actions as a whole—namely,
the Crusades (both in the Middle East and in Europe)—
certainly seem to support this. But it's easy to generalize
when we collapse a millennium into a paragraph or two,
pulling out only the highlights and the lowlights. What
we need to remember, however, is both the big picture
and the small picture.

What has made Christianity so attractive to millions of
people over the past two thousand years is the idea of forgiveness, from Jesus's advice to "turn the other cheek" and
to "love thy neighbor"; to the structure of confession; to the
last rites. Medieval theologians were convinced that hell
existed but also that it wasn't inevitable that anyone would
end up there. Stories such as those of Saint Paul and Saint
Augustine, who converted to Christianity despite their anti-
Christian and hedonistic pasts, were extremely popular—
exemplars of the vast depths of forgiveness available to all.

On the ground, in the day-to-day functioning of Christianity, there was an emphasis on sin, but this was not just
for the sake of dwelling on how awful people could be.
The idea was to be aware of sin, so that a person could confess, repent, and be given a clean slate. This was to make
sure that not only were they, themselves, free of sin but
also that the community ran smoothly.

In the Middle Ages, as now, a person isn't usually expected to be forgiven for something they're not sorry for. A fundamental part of forgiveness is for a person to show contrition, "to amend his faults and not justify his sin."[4] In the monastery, showing contrition was a performance that humbled the person at fault, and it was to be done immediately, even if the guilty brother only suspected he'd offended someone else. According to *The Rule of Saint Benedict*,

> If [a brother] even vaguely senses anger or distress, however minor, of any senior brother's soul toward him, he should at once, without delay, lie prostrate on the ground at his feet, making satisfaction until the disturbance is healed with a blessing.[5]

Reconciliation, not punishment, was the goal: a healing of the relationship between people.

A brother who confessed his sins before he was caught or accused was dealt with more leniently, as this displayed a more penitent heart. A brother who was accused by someone else of having done wrong was in much more hot water, the assumption being that he probably would never have confessed his guilt on his own. Such a brother was more concerned with saving his own skin than healing whomever he'd hurt; his interest was in himself, not his community.

The airing of grievances and sins was one of the items always on the agenda at the daily chapter meetings. Brothers who knew they had wronged another were meant to step up and confess, taking their punishments with grace and humility. Sometimes penance was light, such as repetitions of certain prayers; however, sometimes it was quite brutal, with a brother being stripped to the waist and flogged in front of the community.[6]

Like secular medieval justice (despite its bad reputa-
tion), monastic justice emphasized making amends and
changing a person's ways for the better, both for himself
and for the community. After restitution was made and
penance was given, the sinner was expected to turn over
a new leaf and sin no more. If he continued to make bad
choices that disturbed or disrupted the peace of the monastery, the punishments would escalate. Finally, a brother
who refused to change his behavior was excommunicated
and banished from the monastery. This was done not out
of a sense of revenge or retribution but out of a desire to
preserve the community and protect it from harm. As it
says in *The Rule of Saint Augustine*,

> Should he refuse to submit, let him be ejected from
> your society.... Even this is not done of cruelty, but of
> mercy, lest he ruin many by pestilent infection.

Even within a medieval monastery, forgiveness and
acceptance had to be weighed against the greater good,
and sometimes the greater good meant letting go of a
person who didn't have the community's best interest
at heart.

When it comes to interactions within our own communities, the monastic approach is a helpful model of both
forgiveness and setting healthy boundaries. We all mess
up from time to time and have to apologize and make
amends, especially to those we love and cherish, but
there's a difference between forgiving someone for their
mistakes and having someone take advantage of us. There
is a point at which, no matter how much compassion we
may have for them, keeping certain people close to us
does more harm than good, often to us both.

In the Paternoster, or Lord's Prayer, which monks re-
cited with extreme regularity, is the expectation that ev-

eryone will slip up and require forgiveness from time to time: "Forgive us our trespasses, as we forgive those who trespass against us." A person who has wronged us and shows both true contrition and a willingness to make amends sincerely is a good candidate for our forgiveness. However, we are not required to allow those who are determined to disrupt our lives, damage our self-confidence, or undermine our happiness to remain part of the communities we've built. Like medieval monks, we can remind them that we will still be here if they choose to come back in a way that is constructive, and then we can let them go.

Raise a Glass Every Once in a While

Although we read that wine is not for monks at all, but since in our times monks cannot be persuaded of this, let us at least agree that we should not drink to excess but sparingly.
—Benedict of Nursia, *The Rule of Saint Benedict*

Despite Saint Benedict's disapproval, monasteries produced several different kinds of alcohol, climate permitting. Many European monasteries tended vineyards, which allowed them to make the wine that was such an integral part of their spiritual practice in the form of the Eucharist. Christians were not permitted to use any other liquid in place of wine for this sacrament, which meant it had to be exported to communities far removed from local vineyards. Some monasteries in northern countries like England, however, made do with wine from the symbolic and practical mulberry tree.[7] A sweet addition to the honey and beeswax supplied by an abbey's apiaries was mead, a drink available to people across Europe.

Saint Thomas Becket (pictured in his bishop's miter)
made such tasty beer from his monks' pond water
that he later became the patron saint of the London
Brewers' Company.
The Queen Mary Psalter, fol. 295v, 1310–20 (detail)
British Library, London; Royal 2 B VII

Perhaps the beverage that monasteries are best known
for, however, is beer. In the Middle Ages, beer was locally
produced because of its perishability, and it was brewed
mostly by women in private homes, who sold any excess
to neighbors and townspeople. Monasteries followed this
same pattern on a larger scale, brewing their own beer for
the brothers and their guests, and selling the leftovers.

Although it might seem odd now for religious figures
to be tied to alcohol production, the medieval church
didn't see this as an issue. Beyond the connection of Jesus
to wine, there were plenty of holy ties to drinking, especially surrounding the party saint, Brigid, who not only
turned bathwater into beer but also declared she wanted
to have an entire lake of beer to share with everyone in
heaven—including the Holy Trinity and Mary—as well as
the less fortunate on earth. Another saint, Thomas Becket,
reputedly made such delicious beer from the bathing

*Monks drank both wine and beer,
although they were definitely
not meant to overindulge like
this sneaky brother, as that was
considered to be gluttony.*
Le Régime du corps, fol. 44v,
late 13th century (detail)
British Library, London; Sloane 2435

pond of his monks during his lifetime that he became the patron saint of the London Brewers' Company after his martyrdom.[8]

Beer was a regular part of the monastic diet. The brothers of Barnwell Priory were required "to have daily ready after dinner two jugs of beer for the convent and the guests, whereof one ought to be freshly drawn from the barrel, but the other will be filled with the liquor left in the other jugs." (After all, waste not, want not.) The advice continues,

> When new barrels are filled with beer they are not to be left without someone to watch them. In winter straw is to be placed round the barrels, and, if need be, a fire is to be lighted. In summer the windows of the cellar are to be closed, to prevent the heat of the sun reaching the barrels. The Cellarer [in charge of food and drink] ought not to give new beer to the convent to drink until the fourth day.... On all principal feasts of first dignity, the Cellarer is to provide the convent, for four days, with bread of superior quality, and beer of extra strength.[9]

For obvious reasons, monks were encouraged to practice moderation in their drinking, and while their daily
ration of one gallon of beer each may not seem like a mod-
erate amount to us, it's important to remember that medieval people drank beer from the time they were children,
so their tolerance was quite high, and that beer was both
less alcoholic and more nutritious than it is now.[10]

Beer and moderation don't always go together, however,
and monks were sometimes guilty of overindulging. *The
Penitential of Theodore*, a seventh-century book that out-
lines the penance to be prescribed to a person who sins,
mentions several penalties for drunkenness according to
the monk's rank and the severity of the offense. "Whoever
is drunk against the Lord's command, if he has taken a vow
of sanctity, shall do penance for seven days on bread and
water, or twenty days without fat" (that is, with very bland
food), declares Theodore. However, "if a monk vomits on
account of drunkenness, he shall do penance for thirty
days." Occasionally, though, a monk got off with a lighter
penance, especially if he was a lightweight to begin with:

> If [the offense] is due to weakness or because he has
> been a long time abstinent and is not accustomed to
> drink or eat much; or if it is for gladness at Christmas
> or Easter or for any festival of a saint, and he then had
> imbibed no more than is commanded by his seniors,
> no offence is committed. If a bishop commands it
> no offence is committed, unless he himself does
> likewise.[11]

Given that the cellarer is meant to dole out beer of extra strength on certain feast days, it seems that hangovers
from gladness may have been a fairly common ailment.[12]

Drinking beer might be one of the simplest ways to live
like a monk in the modern age, especially given the many

While Saint Benedict wanted monks to be serious all the time, moments of levity were bound to occur, as with this monk, who risks a smile behind his brother's back.
Biblical psalter, fol. 106r,
c. 13th century (detail)
Walters Art Museum, Baltimore, W.116

beers that claim a connection with monasticism. While there are still monastic brews, such as the famous Trappist beers we drink today, they are not medieval: Trappist beers date back only to the nineteenth century and the reestablishment of monasteries in Belgium.[13] No matter where or when our beer comes from, however, it's best to follow Theodore's advice and not overindulge—or get into a drinking contest with a bishop.

Set Aside Time to Unwind

> *They who love most shall be most blessed, not they who lead the most austere life, for love outweigheth this.*
> —The Ancren Riwle

Believe it or not, medieval religious practice wasn't always serious, wasn't always gloomy, and wasn't always boring. Like brightly colored stained glass windows, tiled floors, painted murals, and illuminated manuscripts, sometimes the activities of the monks could be fun as well. The idea that an eternal lifetime of bliss awaits all believers, worthy or not, is a cause for celebration, so festivals such as Christmas and Easter were meant to be full of the joy to be found in faith and in community.

In addition to voices raised in song,
the ringing of the bells lent its own
joyful music to the monastic day.
Image du Monde, fol. 30v, 1489 (detail)
Walters Art Museum, Baltimore, W.199

Although medieval people didn't put on theatrical plays of the sort that were staged in ancient Greece or the early modern period, we do have records of religious plays being performed, and it seems that they started in the church itself. Simple plays based on the discovery of Jesus's body in the tomb are known to have been performed in the Abbey of Saint Gall, in Switzerland, and Winchester Cathedral, in England, and an injunction against monks for performing plays in England's Tynemouth Priory to celebrate Saint Cuthbert shows that these plays actually were being performed within sacred spaces.[14]

In addition to plays, monks also participated in religious games. One such Easter game involved a ball being tossed back and forth between singers performing a hymn of celebration while the leader of the game stepped through a labyrinth on the floor. Far from irreverent, this ball game in the church was a way in which the brothers could visually demonstrate the power of Jesus over death. As there was only one way to be saved—through faith in Jesus—so there was only one way through the labyrinth. This was not only a fun game, but it was also another way for the monks to meditate on a central tenet of their beliefs.[15]

As we saw in chapter one, the outdoors provided a convenient place for brothers to take a break from the weary-

Although monastic singing was largely done as part of the service, it wasn't always serious. Some songs were used in play as a way of celebrating faith.
Beaupré Antiphonary, vol. 2, fol. 113v, c. 1290
Walters Art Museum, Baltimore; W.760

ing routines of the cloister, too. Despite an abbey's walls, its landholdings meant that even field trips were sometimes a possibility. The prior of Barnwell, for example, was encouraged to take the junior members of the order for the occasional stroll to stretch their legs:

> When…he chooses to visit lands or manors for the
> sake of recreation, he ought to take with him younger
> brethren (now these, now those) for the purpose of
> giving them recreation.[16]

Although the prior surely could use the opportunity to
check on his tenants or teach his companions about the
workings of the monastery and its holdings, neither of
these excuses was strictly necessary. In this case, the walks
were meant to be purely for enjoyment and exercise.

Believe it or not, bloodletting was also a time that
monks could look forward to when they needed a bit of
a rest. Medieval humoral theory, based on the writings of
Galen, who we met earlier, suggested that the body was
made up of four humors: yellow bile, black bile, blood,
and phlegm. Any illness was caused (at least in part) by
these four fluids being out of balance, and so bloodletting
was a way in which the body could be drained of excess
humors in order to restore the balance and therefore the
person's health, both mental and physical.

Monastic tradition required that, unless there was a
compelling reason for someone to abstain, all the brothers in the monastery were to be bled on a regular basis in
order to be kept healthy. As blood donors will know, giving or losing a fair amount of blood leaves the body weak-
ened for a time. In order to make things easier, those who
had been recently bled were permitted a few luxuries that
they might not normally be able to indulge in: namely,
time off work, the ability to speak freely (within reason)
with other monks, and walks in the infirmary garden. Because, naturally, not everyone was bled at the same time, a
brother might send up a quick, self-indulgent prayer to be
on the same schedule as a close friend, so that they might
spend the next two or three days enjoying each other's
company with a little more freedom.

Brothers were meant to undergo bloodletting on a regular basis, but this allowed for time to rest and enjoy the company of friends for a day or two.

Le Régime du corps, fol. 11v, late 13th century (detail) British Library, London; Sloane 2435

When we think about people being devoted to a singular idea, perhaps there is no better example than that of monks and nuns, cloistering themselves away for life in order to contemplate the divine. In our own lives, we may feel driven by a singular goal—wealth, success, fame, security—to the exclusion of all else, or we may be pulled in a million different directions at once. Modern science has shown us that taking breaks is essential to both our happiness and our success in reaching our goals,[17] and it seems that this is something that medieval monks can teach us as well: taking time out for entertainment, for play, and for the sheer joy of movement makes it possible for us to rededicate ourselves to our pursuits with clear minds and happy hearts.

AD MELIORA

Be always doing something from which good may come.

—*The Ancren Riwle*

aving read this far, you've probably already decided that monastic life is not for you. Many people in the Middle Ages made the same realization—hopefully before they took their vows.

Modern scientific study has revealed, unsurprisingly, that living the austere life of a medieval monk is not the way to create a happy life for ourselves. Lack of sleep, a strict diet, a relentless routine, and a near-constant focus on our own failings are not pleasurable, nor particularly healthy ways to live, and pleasure has been shown to be an essential component of happiness.[1] It's important that we bear in mind, however, that pleasure—and even happiness for its own sake—isn't the point of monastic living. The point is to offer oneself completely up to God in a way that is meant to be difficult, in order to show a person's gratitude and devotion; to strip away the self completely in order to become an empty vessel for God's will. For most of us, this is not the goal of our lives, and that is perfectly okay.

What we can learn from monastic life, however, is how to fulfill the other requirement of happiness: living with meaning and purpose. Every moment of a medieval monk's life was imbued with meaning, from the moment he first opened his eyes at the sound of the dormitory bell in the cold midnight hours to the moment he closed them again, tucked modestly away in the rough wool of his homespun hood. Each habit, each ritual, each activity, each interaction was tied to both the service of others and the monk's personal goal of salvation. Fortunately for monks, these two goals were in sync.

Research has shown that we are happiest when we are living in alignment with our personal values and when we are giving of ourselves in the service of others. These activities don't have to be as extreme as monastic rituals to provide us with happy results or to make our communities stronger. We can use our gifts in endless ways to enrich both our lives and the lives of others by following the monastic example, no matter which (if any) faith we believe in: appreciate and spend time in nature; live simply; contemplate our own lives and their meaning; give to others with generosity and empathy; and practice moderation. As medieval monks understood, living and working in harmony with people who support our goals, share our joys, and comfort us in times of need can help us all achieve better lives. But whether we're alone or together, living like a monk—that is, with purpose and compassion—can help us move *ad meliora*: toward better things.

Acknowledgments

Writing a book of advice probably means that you should follow at least some of it, and it brings me great happiness to take a monkish moment to express my gratitude to the people who made this little book possible.

My first words of thanks are owed to the team at Abbeville Press, specifically Lauren Bucca, who not only brought this concept to me but shepherded me through it, despite many obstacles, both global and personal. Little did we know at the outset that we would all soon be living cloistered lives and facing some of the same challenges that medieval monks did!

The inestimable value of a like-minded community has been brought home to me lately, as the community of historians of which I am so lucky to be a part has been a constant source of inspiration and support, especially during this past, difficult year. My thanks especially go to Seb Falk, for kindly setting me straight on my Latin; Peter Konieczny, for always supplying me with research materials and friendship; Charles Spencer, who unknowingly gave me space to write in a literal sense and became a friend in the process; and the many brilliant guests of *The Medieval Podcast* who, week after week, generously share the fruits of their knowledge on air, while also giving me inspiration, encouragement, and wisdom when the microphones are off. I am so incredibly grateful to know you all.

To my podcast listeners, social media followers, and devoted readers, thank you from the bottom of my heart for allowing me to live my dream and for coming with me on the journey. Thanks also to my students and the cocreators of the Medieval Masterclass for Creators, who know better than anyone the challenges and the joys of making a book of your own. Your enthusiasm and support have meant the world to me.

Thank you to my wonderful parents, who never know doubt when it comes to their children's ambitions; to my brilliant brothers and sisters-in-law, whose talents and gifts leave me in awe; and to my amazing nieces and nephews, who think all this medieval stuff is pretty awesome. They are just the tip of the iceberg that is the loving, supportive family I'm privileged and grateful to be part of. My friends, old and new, have been my rock in the stormy seas of the past while, and I have never met such brave, compassionate souls as I have through learning Krav Maga. I love you all immensely and look forward to fighting you again soon.

Finally, thank you to the two dazzlingly beautiful souls who I am eternally grateful to have as my daughters. Your unshakable faith in me, your kindness, your resilience, and your absolute refusal to dim your own brilliant light for any reason are an inspiration to me daily. I am so proud of you.

Saint Benedict would hate this book, as it doesn't sell austerity very well, I know, but I hope I have done some justice to those brothers and sisters whose dedication to their faith was (and still is) rooted in a desire to do good for the people within and without the cloister walls. At the end of many medieval manuscripts is a humble request by the authors and copyists that we readers pray for their souls. In tribute, I'd like to take one last moment to express my gratitude to our medieval monastic brothers and sisters, for setting down their thoughts, struggles, humor, and faith for us to read, and my hope that their souls have found peace.

Notes

AD REGULAM

1. In this section on monastic life in general, I'm indebted to Julie Kerr, whose book *Life in the Medieval Cloister* (New York: Continuum, 2009) contains many of these details. For those who are seeking for a more in-depth look at monastic life, Kerr's book is invaluable.

2. Mary took initial vows at six, which was extremely unusual, following these up with formal vows at twelve; still at least four years shy of the norm. This wasn't her own wish, but that of her grandmother. Mary's father conceded, overruling the express and vehement objections of her mother, Eleanor of Castile. Kelcey Wilson-Lee, *Daughters of Chivalry: The Forgotten Children of Edward I* (London: Picador, 2019), 54, 58.

3. Shannon McSheffrey, "Sanctuary with Shannon McSheffrey," *The Medieval Podcast*, produced by Danièle Cybulskie, January 22, 2020, https://themedievalpodcast.libsyn.com/website/sanctuary-with-shannon-mcsheffrey.

4. John Willis Clark (trans.), *The Observances in Use at the Augustinian Priory of S. Giles and S. Andrew at Barnwell, Cambridgeshire* (Cambridge, UK: Macmillan and Bowes, 1897). Although Augustinians are technically friars, as we'll see throughout this book, the Augustinians at Barnwell Priory were expected to stay within the walls of their monastery like monks, and both their rule and their activities are extremely similar to those of Benedictines. When it comes to outlining daily life in detail, the medieval sources we have are relatively few, so because this is such a richly detailed source, I've chosen to use it to illustrate monastic life here.

5. Clark, *Observances in Use . . . at Barnwell*, 125.

6. Kerr, *Life in the Medieval Cloister*, 110.

1
TEND YOUR PLANTS, AND YOUR SOUL

1. Sylvia Landsberg, *Medieval Gardens* (London: Thames & Hudson, 1996), 36.

2. Paul Meyvaert, "The Medieval Monastic Garden," in *Medieval Gardens*, ed. Elisabeth B. MacDougall (Washington, DC: Dumbarton Oaks, 1986), 45.

3. Landsberg notes that monks considered the Trinity by contemplating "the three states of water, namely the bubbling, sparkling source or spout, the shallow, moving sheet, and the still, silent pool." Landsberg, *Medieval Gardens*, 58–60, 41. See also Meyvaert, "The Medieval Monastic Garden," 52.

4. Tina Bringslimark, Terry Hartig, and Grete Grindal Patil, "Psychological Benefits of Indoor Plants in Workplaces: Putting Experimental Results into Context," *HortScience* 42, no. 3 (June 2007): 581–87, https://doi.org/10.21273/HORTSCI.42.3.581; Roger Ulrich, "Health Benefits of Gardens in Hospitals," paper presented at Plants for People conference, January 2002, https://www.researchgate.net/publication/252307449_Health_Benefits_of_Gardens_in_Hospital.

5. Landsberg, *Medieval Gardens*, 41.

6. Benedict of Nursia, *The Rule of Saint Benedict*, trans. Bruce L. Venarde (Cambridge, MA: Dumbarton Oaks Medieval Library, 2011), 139.

7. For a quick overview of monastic perspectives on meat (including its lusty connotations), fish, and eels, see John Wyatt Greenlee, "Medieval Eels with John Wyatt Greenlee," *The Medieval Podcast*, produced by Danièle Cybulskie, November 1, 2020, https://www.medievalists.net/2020/11/medieval-eels-john-wyatt-greenlee/.

8. Francesco Sofi, Rosanna Abbate, Gian Franco Gensini, Alessandro Casini, "Accruing Evidence on Benefits of Adherence to the Mediterranean Diet on Health: An Updated Systematic Review and Meta-Analysis," *American Journal of Clinical Nutrition* 92, no. 5 (November 2010): 1189–96, https://doi.org/10.3945/ajcn.2010.29673; Richard Hoffman and Mariette Gerber, *The Mediterranean Diet: Health and Science* (Chichester, UK: Wiley-Blackwell, 2012), 1.

9. The efficacy of peppermint oil seems to come from menthol (the name itself derived from the Latin word for "mint"). Babar

Ali, Naser Ali Al-Wabel, Saiba Shams, Aftab Ahamad, Shah Alam Khan, and Firoz Anwar, "Essential Oils Used in Aromatherapy: A Systematic Review," *Asian Pacific Journal of Tropical Biomedicine* 5, no. 8 (August 2015): 601–11, https://doi. org/10.1016/j.apjtb.2015.05.007.

10. Nicholas Everett (trans.), *The Alphabet of Galen: Pharmacy from Antiquity to the Middle Ages* (Toronto: University of Toronto Press, 2014), 231, 38, 201, 147; Faith Wallis, *Medieval Medicine: A Reader* (Toronto: University of Toronto Press, 2010), 103. A review of studies on the antibacterial properties of plants shows promising results on the use of chamomile to aid in healing, especially in the mouth. Other familiar plants, such as oregano, rosemary, and basil, show signs of antibacterial properties too. François Chassagne, Tharanga Samarakoon, Gina Porras, James T. Lyles, Micah Dettweiler, Lewis Marquez, Akram M. Salam, Sarah Shabih, Darya Raschid Farrokhi, and Cassandra L. Quave, "A Systematic Review of Plants with Antibacterial Activities: A Taxonomic and Phylogenetic Perspective," *Frontiers in Pharmacology* 8 (January 2021), https://doi.org/10.3389/fphar.2020.586548.

11. *The Alphabet of Galen* suggests using black mulberry (*Morus nigra*), but it's extract of white mulberry (*Morus alba*) that has been tested and shown to heal burns effectively in rat trials. Landsberg, *Medieval Gardens*, 41; Everett, *Alphabet of Galen*, 291; Nitish Bhatia, Arunpreet Singh, Rohit Sharma, Amandeep Singh, Varinder Soni, Gurjeet Singh, Jaideep Bajaj, Ravi Dhawan, and Balwinder Singh, "Evaluation of Burn Wound Healing Potential of Aqueous Extract of *Morus alba* Based Cream in Rats," *Journal of Phytopharmacology* 3, no. 6 (November–December 2014): 378–83.

12. Clark, *Observances in Use . . . at Barnwell*, 203. Ginger, as we saw, soothed nausea. Among other things, cinnamon was believed to be useful for cough, and peony for epilepsy and nightmares. (Please see your doctor instead of trying these remedies on your own.) Efraim Lev and Zohar Amar, *Practical* Materia Medica *of the Medieval Eastern Mediterranean According to the Cairo Genizah* (Boston: Brill, 2008), 145, 235–36.

13. Peter Damian, "The Monastic Ideal," in *The Portable Medieval Reader*, eds. James Bruce Ross and Mary Martin McLaughlin (New York: Viking Press, 1962), 53.

14. Mary Imelda Horback, "An Annotated Translation of the Life of St. Thomas Becket by Herbert Bosham (Part One)" (master's thesis, Loyola University, 1945), 11; David Townsend, *Saints'*

Lives, vol. 1, *Henry of Avranches* (Cambridge, MA: Dumbarton Oaks Medieval Library, 2014.), 255; Lauren Johnson, *The Shadow King: The Life and Death of Henry VI* (New York: Pegasus Books, 2019), 550.

15. Green burial practices, according to the Green Burial Society of Canada, include "no embalming, direct earth burial, ecological restoration and conservation, communal memorialization, and optimized land use." For this, and a good overview of green burials, please see Chloe Rose Stuart-Ulin, "Green Burials: Everything You Need to Know about the Growing Trend," *CBC*, October 29, 2019, https://www.cbc.ca/life/culture/green-burials-everything-you-need-to-know-about-the-growing-trend-1.5340000.

II
EMBRACE MINIMALISM

1. Elizabeth Gillan Muir, *A Women's History of the Christian Church: Two Thousand Years of Female Leadership* (Toronto: University of Toronto Press, 2019), 81.

2. Quoted in Clark, *Observances in Use ... at Barnwell*, 5.

3. At some monasteries in some moments in time, this was perhaps moot: Seb Falk notes that at Saint Alban's in 1380, twenty-three out of the monastery's fifty-eight monks were named John. Falk, *The Light Ages: The Surprising Story of Medieval Science* (New York: W. W. Norton & Co., 2020), 15. See also Kerr, *Life in the Medieval Cloister*, 59.

4. Benedict, *Rule*, 179–81.

5. In his translation of *The Rule of Saint Benedict*, Bruce L. Venarde suggests that a scapular may have been "an overshirt, smock, or apronlike garment meant to keep other clothes from getting dirty or torn during manual labor." He adds that it may have been hooded. Benedict, *Rule*, 264, 179.

6. Kerr, *Life in the Medieval Cloister*, 45.

7. Marie Kondo, author of *The Life-Changing Magic of Tidying Up* (Berkeley, CA: Ten Speed Press, 2014), insists that clothing is the first category to focus on when we organize our lives, as she believes this is the easiest group of items to make decisions about as to whether or not we need them. Since Saint Benedict would frown upon Kondo's fundamental question for any material object—"Does it spark joy?"—arguing that finding joy in material possessions like clothing is vanity or pride, per-

haps the questions we ask ourselves about why we keep certain items shouldn't be founded upon monastic principles. Kondo, *Life-Changing*, 65.

8. Because medieval people wrote on parchment made of calfskin or sheepskin, taking notes could be a costly activity. Instead, quick notes were written on small wooden or ivory tablets that had a surface covered in beeswax. People would scratch their notes on the wax using a stylus, then scrape, rub, or gently melt the notes off so that the tablet could be used again. The knife in this list was not for defense but for eating with. Benedict, *Rule*, 181.

9. Benedict, *Rule*, 173–75.

10. Jocelin of Brakelond, *Chronicle of the Abbey of Bury St Edmunds*, trans. Diana Greenway and Jane Sayers (Oxford: Oxford University Press, 1989), 102–3. According to the UK National Archives' "Currency Converter: 1270–2017" (https://www.nationalarchives.gov.uk/currency-converter), thirteen shillings in 1270 (the farthest back the converter goes, but still seventy years after John's coronation) would be worth approximately £475 (US$655) today. For a king, then as now, this would not be a particularly generous donation, especially after he had spent at least one night at the abbey with his extensive entourage. Still, it would have been enough to allow the monks to buy a cow or to pay a skilled laborer for sixty-five days of work.

11. Jocelin, *Chronicle*, 35.

12. Benedict, *Rule*, 177.

13. Clark, *Observances in Use . . . at Barnwell*, 121.

14. The idea of being the average of our five closest friends has been attributed not to a scientist but to a motivational speaker, Jim Rohn. However, peer influence has been studied widely, and a few examples include weight loss or gain, physical activity, and divorce, which has even been referred to as "a collective phenomenon." See, respectively: Monica L. Wang, Lori Pbert, and Stephenie C. Lemon, "Influence of Family, Friend and Coworker Social Support and Social Undermining on Weight Gain Prevention among Adults," *Obesity* 22, no. 9 (September 2014): 1973–80, https://doi.org/10.1002/oby.20814; Derek M. Griffith, Andrea King, and Julie Ober Allen, "Male Peer Influence on African American Men's Motivation for Physical Activity: Men's and Women's Perspectives," *American Journal of Men's Health*, November 15, 2012, https://

doi.org/10.1177/1557988312465887; Rose McDermott, James H. Fowler, and Nicholas S. Christakis, "Breaking Up Is Hard to Do, Unless Everyone Else Is Doing It Too: Social Network Effects on Divorce in a Longitudinal Sample," *Social Forces* 92, no. 2 (December 2013): 491–519, https://doi. org/10.1093/sf/sot096.

15. Benedict, *Rule*, 135.

16. For both of these signs, see Alison Ray, "Silence Is a Virtue: Anglo-Saxon Monastic Sign Language," British Library, *Medieval Manuscripts Blog*, November 28, 2016, https://blogs. bl.uk/digitisedmanuscripts/2016/11/silence-is-a-virtue-anglo-saxon-monastic-sign-language.html. While both hearing and deaf people today would likely understand the sign for soap, neither of these is very similar to the modern American Sign Language signs for "soap" or "underwear."

17. Benedict, *Rule*, 147.

18. James Morton (ed. and trans.), *The Ancren Riwle: A Treatise on the Rules and Duties of Monastic Life* (London: J. B. Nichols and Sons, 1853), 89.

19. Benedict, *Rule*, 141.

20. Miranda Olff, Willie Langeland, and Berthold P. R. Gersons, "Effects of Appraisal and Coping on the Neuroendocrine Response to Extreme Stress," *Neuroscience and Biobehavioral Reviews* 29 (2005): 460–61; Paul T. Bartone, Gerald P. Krueger, and Jocelyn V. Bartone, "Individual Differences in Adaptability to Isolated, Confined, and Extreme Environments," *Aerospace Medicine and Human Performance* 89, no. 6 (2018): 540, https://doi.org/10.3357/AMHP.4951.2018.

21. To make positive affirmations hold more weight, think about ways in which they've been shown to be true. Like monks who can point to the fact that they've been forgiven in the past (so they can expect to be forgiven in the future), we know we can be successful because we've already had success in the past. This will help us believe in the truth of our affirmations and set the stage for future success. Tal Ben-Shahar, *Choose the Life You Want: The Mindful Way to Happiness* (New York: Experiment, 2012), 266.

22. Dorie Clark and Seth Godin, "How to Succeed at Creative Work," YouTube video, December 3, 2020, 4:00, recorded for *Newsweek* series *Better*, https://www.youtube.com/watch?v=yaNrcAb-7kg.

23. Benedict did say that the *Rule* was not the last word on all

things monastic; each house would have its own traditions, and exceptions in exceptional cases must be made. However, the *Rule* was definitely meant to be the *first* word on the guidelines for the community.

24. Benedict, *Rule*, 3.

25. James Clear makes a strong case for successful habits being tied to identity, and rituals making this easier. Clear, *Atomic Habits: An Easy and Proven Way to Build Good Habits and Break Bad Ones* (New York: Avery, 2018), 33, 36–37. Tal Ben-Shahar centers these self-affirming rituals as an important contributor to our overall happiness as human beings. Ben-Shahar, *Happier: Learn the Secrets to Daily Joy and Lasting Fulfillment* (New York: McGraw-Hill, 2007), 8–10.

26. Benedict, *Rule*, 57.

III
LOOK INWARD

1. Morton, *Ancren Riwle*, 161.

2. Julian of Norwich, *The Shewings of Julian of Norwich*, ed. Georgia Ronan Crampton (Kalamazoo, MI: Medieval Institute Publications, 2004), 42; translation my own.

3. Caesarius of Heisterbach, *The Dialogue on Miracles*, trans. H. Von E. Scott and C. C. Swinton Bland (New York: Harcourt, Brace and Co., 1929), 47.

4. Julian, *Shewings*, 43.

5. Although the benefits of meditation have been studied extensively, a good summary of the literature, including the seemingly permanent changes in brain function, can be found in Daniel Goleman and Richard Davidson, *Altered Traits: Science Reveals How Meditation Changes Your Mind, Brain, and Body* (New York: Avery Publishing, 2017). For the three-minute breathing exercise, see Mark Williams, John Teasdale, Zindel Segal, and Jon Kabat-Zinn, *The Mindful Way through Depression: Freeing Yourself from Chronic Unhappiness* (New York: Guilford Press, 2007), 182.

6. Quoted in Wallis, *Medieval Medicine*, 82.

7. Medieval Christians believed that the information was worthwhile despite the sources being non-Christian, as decreed by Saint Augustine. For a more thorough look at this, Islamic science in the monastery, and Al-Khwarizmi's name being man-

gled into becoming the word "algorithm," please see Falk, *The Light Ages*, 96, 32.

8. Clark, *Observances in Use ... at Barnwell*, 63, 59.

9. Ibid., 167.

10. Benedict, *Rule*, 163.

11. One of the world's most famous readers, Oprah Winfrey, points to reading as a direct influence on her success: "I can't imagine where I'd be or who I'd be without the essential tool of reading. . . . It gives you the ability to reach higher ground. And keep climbing." Winfrey, *What I Know for Sure* (New York: Flatiron Books, 2014), 26.

12. Walter Isaacson, *Steve Jobs* (New York: Simon and Schuster, 2013), 41.

13. Tal Ben-Shahar puts this succinctly: "The foundation of happiness is first allowing unhappiness." Dorie Clark and Tal Ben-Shahar, "Happiness, Mental Health, and the Holidays," YouTube video, December 17, 2020, 20:23, recorded for *Newsweek* series *Better*, https://www.youtube.com/watch?v=owRGyXpetUA.

14. Morton, *Ancren Riwle*, 339.

15. A readable introduction to this phenomenon, including some relevant studies, is Amelia Aldao, "Why Labeling Emotions Matters: An At-Home Experiment on Emotion Labeling," *Psychology Today*, August 4, 2014, https://www.psychologytoday.com/us/blog/sweet-emotion/201408/why-labeling-emotions-matters.

16. Clark, *Observances in Use ... at Barnwell*, 121; Sara McDougall, "Bastard Priests," *Speculum* 94, no. 1 (January 2019): 146.

17. This phenomenon has been examined by many medieval scholars, including Caroline Walker Bynam and Rudolph M. Bell. Whether or not we find this specific label apt, a connection between spirituality and eating disorders is still evident today, as the many websites dedicated to recovery attest.

18. Caesarius, *Dialogue*, 23.

19. This is a tricky point, in that sometimes a person should be outed in order that his sins may be corrected, as we see monks doing in chapter. At other times, it's inadvisable, as it prejudices the confessor. Caesarius illustrates this in a story of a priest whose concubine had an affair with another man. When the man confessed to the affair, the priest sinned by giving

him too harsh a penance out of a desire to drive the two apart! Caesarius, *Dialogue*, 189.

20. Caesarius, *Dialogue*, 323.

21. As an anchorite, Julian was meant to be considered dead for all intents and purposes anyway, even having been given a spiritual funeral as part of the ritual of enclosure. Writings like *The Ancren Riwle* note that it would be odd to see the dead fraternizing with the living; perhaps Julian's perspective was that the dead, likewise, cannot take credit for their writings.

22. Clark, *Observances in Use ... at Barnwell*, 87.

23. Ben-Shahar, *Happier*, 10.

24. Caesarius, *Dialogue*, 223–24.

25. Clark, *Observances in Use ... at Barnwell*, 205–7.

26. Morton, *Ancren Riwle*, 229.

27. Ben-Shahar, *Happier*, 93; Olff, Langeland, and Gersons, "Effects," 460–61; Bartone, Krueger, and Bartone, "Individual Differences," 540. Rumination has been shown to negatively affect mental health and mood across many studies. According to Katie A. McLaughlin and Susan Nolen-Hoeksema, it "accounts for a significant proportion of the overlap between depression and anxiety in both adolescents and adults." McLaughlin and Nolen-Hoeksema, "Rumination as a Transdiagnostic Factor in Depression and Anxiety," *Behaviour Research and Therapy* 49, no. 3 (March 2011): 186–93, https://doi.org/10.1016/j.brat.2010.12.006.

IV
LOOK OUTWARD

1. Nicholas Orme, *Medieval Children* (New Haven, CT: Yale University Press, 2003), 227.

2. Clark, *Observances in Use ... at Barnwell*, 175.

3. Orme, *Medieval Children*, 227.

4. Levi Roach, "Forgeries in the Middle Ages with Levi Roach," *The Medieval Podcast*, produced by Danièle Cybulskie, February 18, 2021, https://themedievalpodcast.libsyn.com/forgeries-in-the-middle-ages-with-levi-roach.

5. Jocelin, *Chronicle*, 36.

6. Ibid., 94–97.

7. In many cases, it was unnecessary to install a town clock be-
    cause the ringing of the church bells kept everyone within
    hearing range on track anyway.

8. As the centuries passed, monks began to keep track of *both* the
    canonical hours and the sixty-minute hours that have since
    become a global standard, using clocks, astrolabes, and other
    methods. For a readable and thorough look at timekeeping as
    well as the many ways in which scientific innovation and mo-
    nastic life and thought went hand in hand in the Middle Ages,
    laying the foundation for modern culture, please see Falk, *The
    Light Ages*.

9. Carole Rawcliffe, "A Marginal Occupation? The Medieval
    Laundress and Her Work," *Gender and History* 21, no. 1 (April
    2009), 151, https://doi.org/10.1111/j.1468-0424.2009.01539.x.

10. Carole Rawcliffe, *Urban Bodies: Communal Health in Late
    Medieval English Towns and Cities* (Woodbridge, UK: Boydell
    Press, 2013), 313–39; Orme, *Medieval Children*, 86.

11. Nuns also created books, as the discovery of traces of blue
    paint on a medieval nun's teeth confirms. Anita Radini, Mon-
    ica Tromp, Alison Beach, E. Tong, Camilla Speller, Michael
    McCormick, J. V. Dudgeon, Matthew Collins, F. Rühli, Roland
    Kroeger, and Christina Warinner, "Medieval Women's Early
    Involvement in Manuscript Production Suggested by Lapis
    Lazuli Identification in Dental Calculus," *Science Advances* 5,
    no. 1 (January 2019), doi:10.1126/sciadv.aau7126.

12. For a closer look at medieval manuscripts and how they were
    made, please see Christopher de Hamel, *Medieval Craftsmen:
    Scribes and Illuminators* (Toronto: University of Toronto Press,
    1992).

13. As Jack Hartnell puts it, "The mouth was a key point of contact
    for the sacred to flow back and forth." Hartnell, *Medieval Bodies:
    Life and Death in the Middle Ages* (New York: W. W. Norton &
    Co., 2018), 75.

V

EVERYTHING IN MODERATION, INCLUDING MODERATION

1. Morton, *Ancren Riwle*, 219.

2. Caesarius, *Dialogue*, 242.

3. Morton, *Ancren Riwle*, 423

4. Clark, *Observances in Use ... at Barnwell*, 131.

5. Benedict, *Rule*, 225.

6. Kerr, *Life in the Medieval Cloister*, 122–23.

7. Noëlle Phillips, *Craft Beer Culture and Modern Medievalism: Brewing Dissent* (Leeds, UK: Arc Humanities Press, 2020), 29.

8. Brigid also was able to create butter from nettles and bacon from bark; for these miracles and bathwater beer, see Mary Wellesley, "Exploding Eyes, Beer from Bath-Water and Butter from Nettles," British Library, *Medieval Manuscripts Blog*, February 1, 2016, https://blogs.bl.uk/digitisedmanuscripts/2016/02/exploding-eyes-beer-from-bath-water-and-butter-from-nettles-the-extraordinary-life-of-brigid-of-kild.html." See Phillips, *Craft*, for the lake of beer (22–23), Thomas Becket (28–29), and an in-depth discussion about monastic beer and culture, then and now.

9. Clark, *Observances in Use ... at Barnwell*, 155, 185.

10. Phillips, *Craft*, 30.

11. Theodore of Tarsus, "The Penitential of Theodore," in *Readings in Medieval History*, ed. Patrick J. Geary (Peterborough, ON: Broadview Press, 1989), 277.

12. The *Observances* of Barnwell Priory mention that people who are hungover should take some time off with the same restful cures prescribed for sadness we saw in chapter three. Clark, *Observances in Use ... at Barnwell*, 207.

13. Phillips, *Craft*, 31.

14. David Bevington, *Medieval Drama* (Boston, MA: Houghton Mifflin, 1975), 26–29; Falk, *The Light Ages*, 181.

15. Max Harris, *Sacred Folly: A New History of the Feast of Fools* (Ithaca, NY: Cornell University Press, 2011), 54–62.

16. Clark, *Observances in Use ... at Barnwell*, 49.

17. Tal Ben-Shahar likens this to building muscle: recovery time is essential in order to effectively deal with stress and be more productive. Clark and Ben-Shahar, "Happiness, Mental Health," 12:22.

AD MELIORA

1. Ben-Shahar, *Happier*, 36.

Glossary

abbess The woman in charge of a community of nuns. In monasteries that housed both monks and nuns, abbesses (not abbots) were usually put in charge. For the etymology, please see **abbot**.

abbey The buildings and grounds of an enclosed community of monks, nuns, or both. See also **convent, monastery**.

abbot The man in charge of a community of monks. Although the *Oxford English Dictionary* notes that the etymology of the word is disputed, in his *Rule*, Saint Benedict suggests that "abbot" comes from Romans 8:15, "We cry out Abba, Father." The abbot was to be a father figure to the brothers.

accidie Depression and listlessness associated with the monastic life. Accidie (also spelled "acedia") was sinful, leading as it did to sloth, doubt, and despair. Brothers who were suffering from accidie were meant to rest and take time off from their duties until their mental health was restored.

almoner The person in charge of the monastery's charitable works, such as distributing alms and food to the needy and watching over students.

anchorite A person who permanently enclosed themselves in a cell (**anchor-hold**) attached to a church in order to remove themselves from the world and dedicate themselves to spiritual practice. Anchorites could be of any gender.

Augustinians Friars who followed *The Rule of Saint Augustine* as their guide.

Benedictines Monks who followed *The Rule of Saint Benedict* as their guide.

canonical hours The times each day during which clergy and the devout were meant to worship using specific prayers and hymns. These were spread out according to the length of daylight, not the sixty-minute hours we use today. The names of these services were matins, lauds, prime, terce, sext, none, vespers, and compline. Monks and nuns were sometimes commissioned to create books of hours for the devotion of private citizens.

cellarer The person in charge of food and drink at the abbey.

chapter The daily meeting to discuss the business of the abbey. These meetings were held in the **chapter house** and included all monks or nuns but excluded novices and lay brothers and sisters.

choir The part of the church where monks performed their religious services.

church fathers Christian writers whose wisdom the faithful would turn to for guidance in matters of theology, especially thorny questions, such as whether or not pagan books should be studied. Two of these theological heavyweights were Saint Jerome and Saint Augustine.

Cistercians Monks who followed *The Rule of Saint Benedict* with extreme strictness and austerity, following the example of their motherhouse at Cîteaux, France. They frequently wore undyed white robes, and aimed to live in communities that were as self-sustaining and remote as possible.

clerk A man educated by the church, but who has not been ordained as a priest or taken vows as a monk.

cloister The buildings exclusive to the monks and nuns within the **precinct**. These buildings normally included a **dormitory**, **refectory**, and **chapter house** and were arranged in a square or rectangle around a **garth**, with the church making up one side.

Cluniacs Monks who followed *The Rule of Saint Benedict* with some relaxed modifications, following the example of their motherhouse at Cluny, France. Because their services were much longer and more extensive than those of other monastic orders, they spent more time in the church and less in manual labor.

convent The buildings and grounds of an enclosed community of monks, nuns, or both. See also **abbey, monastery**.

cowl A hood that covered the head and shoulders.

dormitory The large room in which the monks slept.

Eucharist The sacrament in which wine and bread blessed by a priest are transformed into the body and blood of Jesus during the Mass.

friar A man who has taken vows similar to those of a monk (poverty, chastity, and obedience) but whose order does not necessarily require him to be cloistered. Friars often spent their time in the community instead, preaching and converting people to Christianity. Augustinians, Franciscans, and Dominicans are not monks, but friars.

garth The square or rectangular green space in the center of the **cloister**.

Gothic A type of decoration and architecture that began in the twelfth century, characterized by ornate design and embellishment driven by religious devotion. The cathedral of Notre-Dame de Paris is considered to be a prime example of Gothic architecture.

habit The clothing of a monk or nun, based on simple medieval garments.

hermit A person who retreats from civilization in order to devote themselves to religious practice.

lay brother/lay sister A member of a monastic community who may have taken some vows but is not a full monk or nun. These support staff lived on the monastery's grounds and helped provide for the community by contributing skilled labor or service.

mendicant A member of a religious order who is not required to live in a monastery but is encouraged to support themselves by begging. The orders of Saint Francis and Saint Dominic are mendicant orders.

monastery The buildings and grounds of an enclosed community of monks, nuns, or both. See also **abbey, convent**.

monk A man who has taken vows of poverty, chastity, and obedience, and who is a permanent member of an enclosed community.

novice A new member of a monastic community, who must spend a year living in the abbey and learning about its rules and rituals before being permitted to take vows. This probationary period is called a **novitiate**.

nun A woman who has taken vows of poverty, chastity and obedience, and who is a permanent member of an enclosed community.

oblate A child who is given to a monastic community to be raised.

penance The task or tasks a sinner must complete before their sins are completely absolved. Common examples of penance involved repeating prayers or fasting.

pilgrim A person who travels to visit a religious site. Medieval pilgrims commonly visited the **shrines** of saints in order to pray for aid, give thanks, or perform **penance**. They believed that holy **relics** held the power to help them in their need.

precinct The buildings and grounds enclosed by a monastery's walls.

priory A monastic house run by a prior or prioress, the second in command to an **abbot** or **abbess**. These would have been under the supervision of an abbot or abbess at a separate motherhouse.

purgatory The place where souls that were not consigned to hell but not yet permitted to enter heaven were to wait until time had worn away their sins. Medieval Christians believed that prayers lessened loved ones' time in purgatory, so they frequently made donations to monasteries to have monks and nuns help the dead through prayer.

refectory A monastery's dining hall.

regular clergy People who lived according to a religious rule (*regula*). These included monks, nuns, friars, and members of the military orders such as Templars and Hospitallers.

relic A physical object with holy origins, believed to have the power to perform miracles. These were typically the bones of saints, but other relics included Jesus's crown of thorns, pieces of his cross, and even drops of the Virgin Mary's breast milk. Relics were kept in dedicated containers called **reliquaries** that often took the shape of the relic itself, such as an arm, a foot, or even a head.

sacrament One of the major religious rites that serve as pillars to Christian faith. These include baptism, the Eucharist, marriage, and taking holy orders, among others.

sacrist The person in charge of the objects used in the Mass, including the dishes for the bread and wine of the Eucharist. The sacrist also rang the bells—or directed others to ring the bells—to announce services.

sanctuary The inside of the church. Also, a state in which a person is safe from prosecution and bodily harm. People who had committed crimes or were fleeing violence could claim sanctuary on holy ground, such as a church, churchyard, or monastery. They could not set foot off these grounds afterward, however, or they could immediately be arrested or once again vulnerable to their enemies. Sanctuary seekers were sometimes unintended members of the larger monastic community.

scriptorium The room in which monks wrote, copied, and illuminated books.

secular clergy Members of the religious community who live and work in the outside world. These include clerks, priests, bishops, and archbishops.

shrine A placed dedicated to **relics**.

theologians Religious thinkers.

tonsure The shaved circle at the crown of a religious man's head, worn by both **secular** and **regular clergy**. The origins of the tonsure are debated. It's likely this shaving began as a rejection of sexuality, but Saint Thomas Aquinas praised tonsures because they resemble crowns and, being circles, are the perfect shape. To Aquinas, this made them a fitting symbol for those who sought spiritual perfection and a heavenly crown.

Recommended Reading

Benedict of Nursia. *The Rule of Saint Benedict*. Translated by Bruce L. Venarde. Cambridge, MA: Dumbarton Oaks Medieval Library, 2011.

Ben-Shahar, Tal. *Choose the Life You Want: The Mindful Way to Happiness*. New York: Experiment, 2012.

———. *Happier: Learn the Secrets to Daily Joy and Lasting Fulfillment.* New York: McGraw-Hill, 2007.

Bevington, David. *Medieval Drama*. Boston, MA: Houghton Mifflin, 1975.

Biller, Peter, and A. J. Minnins, eds. *Medieval Theology and the Natural Body*. York, UK: York Medieval Press, 1997.

Caesarius of Heisterbach. *The Dialogue on Miracles*. Translated by H. Von E. Scott and C. C. Swinton Bland. New York: Harcourt, Brace and Co., 1929.

Clark, John Willis, trans. *The Observances in Use at the Augustinian Priory of S. Giles and S. Andrew at Barnwell, Cambridgeshire*. Cambridge, UK: Macmillan and Bowes, 1897.

Clear, James. *Atomic Habits: An Easy and Proven Way to Build Good Habits and Break Bad Ones*. New York: Avery, 2018.

Cullum, P. H. and Katherine J. Lewis. *Holiness and Masculinity in the Middle Ages*. Toronto: University of Toronto Press, 2005.

Damian, Peter. "The Monastic Ideal." In *The Portable Medieval Reader*, edited by James Bruce Ross and Mary Martin McLaughlin, 49–55. New York: Viking Press, 1962.

De Hamel, Christopher. *Medieval Craftsmen: Scribes and Illuminators*. Toronto: University of Toronto Press, 1992.

Everett, Nicholas, trans. *The Alphabet of Galen: Pharmacy from Antiquity to the Middle Ages; A Critical Edition of the Latin Text with English Translation and Commentary*. Toronto: University of Toronto Press, 2014.

Falk, Seb. *The Light Ages: The Surprising Story of Medieval Science*. New York: W. W. Norton & Co., 2020.

Goleman, Daniel, and Richard Davidson. *Altered Traits: Science Reveals How Meditation Changes Your Mind, Brain, and Body.* New York: Avery Publishing, 2017.

Harris, Max. *Sacred Folly: A New History of the Feast of Fools.* Ithaca, NY: Cornell University Press, 2011.

Hartnell, Jack. *Medieval Bodies: Life and Death in the Middle Ages.* New York: W. W. Norton & Co., 2018.

Hoffman, Richard, and Mariette Gerber. *The Mediterranean Diet: Health and Science.* Chichester, UK: Wiley-Blackwell, 2012.

Horback, Mary Imelda. "An Annotated Translation of the Life of St. Thomas Becket by Herbert Bosham (Part One)." Master's thesis, Loyola University, 1945. https://ecommons.luc.edu/cgi/viewcontent.cgi?article=1214&context=luc_theses.

Isaacson, Walter. *Steve Jobs.* New York: Simon and Schuster, 2013.

Jocelin of Brakelond. *Chronicle of the Abbey of Bury St Edmunds.* Translated by Diana Greenway and Jane Sayers. Oxford: Oxford University Press, 1989.

Johnson, Lauren. *The Shadow King: The Life and Death of Henry VI.* New York: Pegasus Books, 2019.

Julian of Norwich. *The Shewings of Julian of Norwich.* Edited by Georgia Ronan Crampton. Kalamazoo, MI: Medieval Institute Publications, 2004.

Kerr, Julie. "Health and Safety in the Medieval Monasteries of Britain." *History* 93, no. 1 (January 2008): 3–19.

———. *Life in the Medieval Cloister.* New York: Continuum, 2009.

Kondo, Marie. *The Life-Changing Magic of Tidying Up.* Berkeley, CA: Ten Speed Press, 2014.

Landsberg, Sylvia. *Medieval Gardens.* London: Thames & Hudson, 1996.

Lev, Efraim, and Zohar Amar. *Practical* Materia Medica *of the Medieval Eastern Mediterranean According to the Cairo Genizah.* Boston: Brill, 2008.

McMillan, Douglas J., and Kathryn Smith Fladenmuller. *Regular Life: Monastic, Canonical, and Mendicant Rules.* Kalamazoo, MI: Medieval Institute Publications, 1997.

Melville, Gert. *The World of Medieval Monasticism: Its History and Forms of Life.* Collegeville, MN: Liturgical Press, 2016.

Meyvaert, Paul. "The Medieval Monastic Garden." In *Medieval Gardens*, edited by Elisabeth B. MacDougall, 23–54. Washington, DC: Dumbarton Oaks, 1986.

Morton, James, ed. and trans. *The Ancren Riwle: A Treatise on the Rules and Duties of Monastic Life.* London: J. B. Nichols and Sons, 1853.

Muir, Elizabeth Gillan. *A Women's History of the Christian Church: Two Thousand Years of Female Leadership.* Toronto: University of Toronto Press, 2019.

Orme, Nicholas. *Medieval Children.* New Haven, CT: Yale University Press, 2003.

Phillips, Noëlle. *Craft Beer Culture and Modern Medievalism: Brewing Dissent.* Leeds, UK: Arc Humanities Press, 2020.

Rawcliffe, Carole. *Urban Bodies: Communal Health in Late Medieval English Towns and Cities.* Woodbridge, UK: Boydell Press, 2013.

Theodore of Tarsus. "The Penitential of Theodore." In *Readings in Medieval History*, edited by Patrick J. Geary, 276–98. Peterborough, ON: Broadview Press, 1989.

Townsend, David. *Saints' Lives.* Vol. 1. *Henry of Avranches.* Cambridge, MA: Dumbarton Oaks Medieval Library, 2014.

Wallis, Faith. *Medieval Medicine: A Reader.* Toronto: University of Toronto Press, 2010.

Williams, Mark, John Teasdale, Zindel Segal, and Jon Kabat-Zinn. *The Mindful Way through Depression: Freeing Yourself from Chronic Unhappiness.* New York: Guilford Press, 2007.

Wilson-Lee, Kelcey. *Daughters of Chivalry: The Forgotten Children of Edward I.* London: Picador, 2019.

Winfrey, Oprah. *What I Know For Sure.* New York: Flatiron Books, 2014.

Index

Illustration Credits